The HEADSTONE

Building the House of God!
God's Apostolic Mandate For the Conclusion of all things in Christ!

*"...and He shall bring forth the Headstone
with shoutings, crying Grace, Grace unto it."*

FAITH MARIE BACZKO

ISBN – 9798325484650

Email: contact@faithmariebaczko.ca

Website: www.faithmariebaczko.ca

Cover design by Edgar Winter

edgarwinter@gmail.com

The Headstone Series is dedicated to my precious son,

Jesse Jordan Robinson.

Both Jesse and I have paid the tremendous cost of birthing this work in the

refining fire of God's Love.

Jesse died on September 10th, 2006 in a fatal car accident.

He was twenty-four years old.

The Fruit of this ministry is accredited to Jesse as

his inheritance in Christ.

THIS SERIES IS A TRIBUTE TO:

My Heavenly Father, the One to whom I have always been able to run to, pour out my heart every day, and receive nothing in return but love. I offer this work back to You as a sacrifice of love to be used in the fulfillment of Your plans and purposes.

To Jesus my LORD, my King and Lover of my soul—the One who made it all possible by His Precious Blood. Your face is the face I long to see. May these works glorify Your Great Name and bring You honour wherever they are taught. Blessing, Honour, Glory, and Power belong to You alone forever and ever, for You alone are worthy.

To the most precious Holy Spirit, I have no adequate words to describe the depth of gratitude in my heart for You. You have been my Teacher and my Friend during the times I felt alone, my Comforter through the painful times; the One who gently and lovingly encouraged me to keep going when I wanted to quit, and who picked me up and carried me when I could not stand. I do not know how to express how much I love you, but I thank You from the very depths of my heart.

ACKNOWLEDGEMENTS

With deep appreciation, I extend my heartfelt gratitude to the remarkable apostolic women whose resolute spirits and unwavering dedication have illuminated the path for this unique and historic generation of women to whom this book is dedicated. Your enduring legacy serves as a beacon of inspiration, guiding us through the corridors of faith, resilience, and empowerment.

To the trailblazers who fearlessly challenged norms, shattered glass ceilings, and embraced their divine calling with grace and courage, your contributions have not only left an indelible mark on the tapestry of history but have worked to shape our collective journey.

May this dedication serve as a humble homage to the extraordinary women who have forged paths of righteousness, compassion, and transformation. To the apostolic women, past, present, and future, your influence has been an e gift, and for that, I express my deepest gratitude and admiration.

CONTENTS

SECTION IV – PREPARE THE WAY

PREFACE
THE HEADSTONE SERIES

"He shall bring forth the *headstone* thereof with shoutings,
Crying, Grace, grace unto it." Zechariah 4-7 KJV

The Headstone Series showcases facets of the brilliant and priceless Gem Stone that is our God. These are facets He will have restored and presented in their fullness, to be reflected in the House prepared for His Son's return. The Headstone generation is being perfected to work with God in the 11th hour for this Holy endeavor! The Headstone or Capstone of the temple of God represents the perfecting work of God in His people to bring them into the fullness of the Glory and majesty of Christ. The Headstone corresponds to the Holy of Holies—the Sanctuary the Holy Spirit is preparing for the Lord's return, to host the Ark of His Presence. It embodies a generation called forth for such a time, to carry the weight of His Glory and prepare His way.

In the Headstone, the great mystery of God's handiwork throughout the ages is unveiled to principalities and powers. The Headstone reveals to all, the manifold wisdom of God and the dynamics of a multidimensional God in perfect union with the *sons of God.* It depicts the prepared Bride united with Christ in completion.

"Now look at the jewel I have set before Jeshua, a single stone with seven facets. I will engrave an inscription on it, says the LORD of Heaven's Armies, and I will remove the sins of this land in a single day." Zechariah 3:9 NLT

The Bride of Christ can be likened to a magnificent Diamond cut and shaped by God the Master Craftsman; designed to reflect the multifaceted and multidimensional virtues and attributes of Almighty God. She is a precious Stone, purchased at a great cost to Him. Fashioned and formed under great pressure in the fire of His Love, she emerges a most outstanding, prized, and unique stone brought forth for His Royal Diadem for such a time!

Set against the backdrop of the darkness of the world, she lights up in a kaleidoscope of wonder and color. As the fiery Light of His Love touches her, her brilliance shoots forth its dancing rays of His Great Glory, enticing the world to approach and drink of this great marvel... *"That you may drink deeply and be delighted with the abundance of her glory" (Is. 66:11).*

God is at work to bring this about! Many important features of the early Church are presently being restored and God is bringing fresh revelation on key doctrines—all working to prepare the Body of Christ for great moves of God on the horizon. Every work that God has birthed in the past or is presently birthing, to enhance the building work of His House is important to the completion of His House—each contributes its 'part,' *"For we know in part and we prophesy in part" (1Cor. 13:9).*

The measure that the House of God is structured according to the Father's design—whether individually or corporately—*determines the measure of His Glory it will reflect.* God has been at work over time, building His House, precept upon precept, by the Body's ability to appropriate and process revelation. With the Body's apprehension of revelation and truth, and a grasp of its identity as *one entity* conformed to the very image of Christ, comes the level of Glory it will appropriate—through God's process the Body is being transformed in a continuous movement from one level of the Glory of God to another.

"In Him the whole structure is joined (bound, welded together harmoniously, and it continues to rise (grow, increase) into a holy temple in the Lord [a sanctuary dedicated, consecrated, and sacred to the presence of the Lord]." Ephesians 2:21 AMP

The Headstone is the culmination of four thousand years of God's work (beginning with Abraham) refined and perfected in the last days in a body of servants. The building of the Headstone is established and purposed to come forth in the Power and the might of the Holy Spirit, in the timing of the apostolic age—the final stage of the building of God's Temple.

The Headstone represents a revolutionary apostolic people led by a God-ordained authentic apostolic government united with Christ and firmly established by God. These will work with Him to establish His plans and purposes in the nations through all spheres and systems of society in the last days. These servants will walk like Christ, doing and saying only what the Father is doing and saying, they will work with God to prepare a Bride for Union with Christ.

The coming forth of the Headstone is Heaven's release of a prepared apostolic people who are bold enough to believe God, ones who will rule and reign with Him *now* to establish His purposes for the ages *to come*! The Headstone Series intends to bring revelation and understanding of *Yahweh's design of His House*—the structure *He intended* to house His Presence and carry the fullness of His Glory. Each of the books in *The Headstone Series* represents a facet of Yahweh's House important to its completion, facets such as Holiness, Israel, women, Heaven's warfare, Union, and our identity as sons of God.

God began to download revelation and understanding of *the Headstone* twenty years ago, releasing me to begin to write the series 2000. However, it was in 2012 that He allowed me to begin to prepare the books for publication, seven have now been published with one more to follow.

Faith Marie Baczko

INTRODUCTION

The building of God's Temple is God's work and Divinely ordered! The blueprint of His House emanated from His heart and His mind. God's plan has always been for His apostolic servants to work alongside Him, following His lead and adhering to His instructions. The Blueprint and pattern of this Temple are *'The Christ'* and only Christ. All that is not of Christ will be shaken free from His Body, burned up, and destroyed in the refining fire of the end-times (1 Cor. 3:11-13). Approaching this work with passion, in the fear of the Lord, and with holy hands is imperative.

As believers in God, we can see and grasp *Truth* only in proportion to the amount of Light we are presently living and walking in. Pride is the condition that hinders our vision and measures our response to the Light of Christ. Many Christians today have ears to hear but do not hear, and eyes to see but do not see (Mark 8:18).

The Scriptures teach that we are continually being changed from "*glory to glory*" and are therefore continuously receiving greater understanding and revelation as we travel towards the Light of Glory in Christ, and as we grow in maturity. Not until Christ appears will we fully know Him as He is. We presently see only *'in part'* and will not fully *'see'* until we see Him face to face. This means that everyone is presently living and functioning under a certain level of darkness. Those who do *see in part*, see in direct proportion to their level of consecration and separation unto God. They see in proportion to their humility and level of brokenness, as pride *always* blinds and prevents us from seeing and hearing.

It is possible to utilize our maximum range of vision, seeing one hundred percent of the view before us from a certain position, only to discover that we have been missing important parts of a magnificent picture when we move from our position and step closer to the Light. Sometimes, a door is then opened to us that we did not previously know existed, or a new factor is introduced into the equation, bringing with it greater understanding. This is the reason Paul prayed for the Church, that the eyes of its heart would be enlightened to receive *and continue* to receive greater and greater revelation and further understanding of the knowledge of Christ (Eph. 1:17-18).

As we mature and progress on our journey towards the Light, the Holy Spirit, our Teacher guides us carefully into a greater spiritual understanding of concepts and ideas born in the Mind of an Omnipotent and Omniscient God. For every bit of Light that God gives us, we are expected to respond to it. We are responsible for pressing into that Light and continuing to move forward into Glory; otherwise, we run the risk of losing the Light He gives and remain in a stationary position, *never growing or progressing in the Lord.*

When guiding those who serve as leaders, God employs straightforward and relatable examples to unveil Heavenly Spiritual concepts beyond our earthly comprehension. These natural and simple illustrations are designed to bridge the gap, making these profound truths accessible and understandable to us. As He said:

> *"For My thoughts are not your thoughts, nor are your ways My ways," says the LORD. "For as the heavens are higher than the earth, so are My ways higher than your ways, and My thoughts than your thoughts." Isaiah 55:8-9*

> *"But the natural man does not receive the things of the Spirit of God, for they are foolishness to him; nor can he know them because they are spiritually discerned." 1Corinthians 2:14*

When conveying knowledge that surpasses an individual's current understanding, an effective teaching approach entails breaking down complex concepts into more digestible components. This entails presenting a sequence of simple ideas and vivid images that progressively guide the learner toward deeper dimensions of truth. The ultimate objective is the development of the capacity to grasp the concept in its entirety. This method, when guided by God's divine wisdom, navigates the disciple through a journey of transformation, shifting the pilgrim from the tangible aspects of the natural world toward spiritual understanding. The ultimate aim is to cultivate a profound comprehension of the 'Mind of Christ' and His essence.

The Word of God is a compilation of stories of true historical accounts, using analogies, metaphors, and parables, possessing the supernatural ability to teach us simple truths, yet has the Divine capacity to continue to release the greater revelation of the depths of God. God teaches us through images and analogies such as Land, a City, a Body, a Bride, a Temple, Kings, and Kingdoms. These examples each have locked within them seeds of God-sized concepts. These analogies bring with them illumination and understanding of God's purposes and thoughts towards man, as He takes each from its simplest form and expands its depth, breadth, and height until the revelation emerges unveiled in all its fullness and Glory.

We may be able to have the mind of Christ on certain issues, for direction, and in a measure directly related to the level of our consecration to Him, but until He comes, we *"know in part and we prophesy in part"* (1 Cor.13:9). The depths of God and the mysteries of His Word are available to any leader who is willing to pay the cost of mining the unfathomable, as these priceless treasures are 'hidden in darkness.' (Is. 45).

A macrocosm is the all-encompassing entirety of an intricate structure, exemplified by the vastness of the universe. It provides *a comprehensive view of the grand plan.* In contrast, a microcosm serves as a miniature representation, complete in itself yet intricately linked to the larger reality.

A single cell of a body could be described as a microcosm—a microscopic unit of an organism; the organism or body being the macrocosm. This principle is woven into Creation by God. The principles and laws that govern the universe hold true for the tiniest natural particle. This is also true in the realm of the Spirit regarding spiritual concepts. Every component fits together in fractal perfection.

The Kingdom of God or the Promised Land of Christ, with all that, that encompasses are but macrocosmic reflections of God's unfolding plan on Earth. Man is but a microcosm or individual cell of the local church, the Church of a given nation, and the global Church—*the Body of Christ.* The macrocosm is the Body of Christ filled with the Holy Spirit, occupying, filling, and ruling the world, the universe, and the heavenly realms in and with Christ (Eph. 4:10).

During my initial experiences learning to drive, my instructor shared invaluable advice that has remained etched in my memory and has proven beneficial for growth in many circumstances. He saw that I was looking too closely in front of me and consequently not driving very well. He advised me to look toward the farthest point of the horizon, take in the entire picture before me, and then simply drive forward. In the same way, there are times when it is important to take note of where we are, especially when we are about to change direction. However, a clear perspective of where we are, where we are going, and how everything fits into the macrocosm—the larger picture God is painting, must always be maintained.

Looking too closely before us hinders our ability to grasp the broader landscape, hindering our navigation of the path ahead. This tendency in the Body of Christ, not only hinders correct forward movement but also causes disunity, as leaders may become absorbed in their own revelations and perceptions, each limited by their perspective and narrow field of vision. When the emphasis shifts towards defending personal positions and dissecting the revelations rather than pursuing the unfathomable and surpassing majesty of Christ, the risk arises of becoming closed-minded. In such a state, one becomes incapable of perceiving, hearing, or understanding anything beyond the confines of their narrow viewpoint.

It takes great humility to put revelation on the altar for the sake of unity, the health of the Body, and the greater cause of love in Christ's purposes. It is important to God that His leaders embrace the revelation of others that He has put His seal on and is impacting with His Spirit. Only when there is maturity can this occur. Humble hearts will then be opened to see all *the parts* fitting together to form a much greater and much more magnificent revelation than may have been previously understood.

The *Headstone Series* of books attempts to do this—stepping back to embrace the *larger revelation* with the full acknowledgment that everything cannot be seen. Greater Light will come and therefore greater revelation as God blesses our unity with the Spirit of wisdom and revelation in the knowledge of Him (Eph. 1:17). These books are an attempt to show the Macrocosm, with revelations that may not have been seen before. It showcases the Temple of God, built with the Hands of God from its foundation to its completion in Glory. This is revealed progressively through the chapters of this book, (see also our book *The Blueprint*).

We are about to embark on a journey towards the *bigger picture* using the many Biblical analogies God has provided for us to aid us in our understanding of these

God-sized concepts, and to bring us to an understanding of where we are in God's *kairos* appointed time.

The Turmoil that the world presently faces in the twenty-first century, the signs occurring in Israel, the great release of women in leadership roles, the momentum gained in worldwide intercession, the greater understanding of spiritual warfare, the movement to fast and worship; the release of prophets and apostles, and the many notable revivals occurring in the last few decades, taken collectively are sure signs that we have entered into the *fullness of time*—a period of transitioning into the Kingdom Age.

This transitional period will be very unstable, unpredictable, and turbulent—a time when the Earth will rock and shake under the weight of thousands of years of transgression. To navigate the way ahead with wisdom through this very unsettling time, the Body will need to first release all control to the Lord. He is the only One who can steer us through this time and get us home safely, *"for you have not passed this way before"* (Josh. 3:4).

The coming forth of the Bride has been occurring in stages over the millennia through many traumatic and violent events. She is coming into the fullness of God to completion as we move toward the most violent and turbulent time in the history of the world—*the birth of a new era.* These violent labor pains are working to give birth to the last dispensation of the Bride's formation. It is therefore vital that we understand this stage of her development and her completion in preparation for the Bridegroom's Return. Join me as we move through history, positioned to see the larger picture with a fresh perspective of God's unfolding plan.

SECTION I

YAHWEH'S HOUSE

"Son of man, describe the temple to the house of Israel,

that they may be ashamed of their iniquities;

and let them measure the pattern.

And if they are ashamed of all that they have done,

make known to them the design of the temple

and its arrangement, its exits and its entrances,

its entire design and all its ordinances,

all its forms, and all its laws. Write it down in their sight,

so that they may keep its *whole design* and all its ordinances,

and perform them. This is the law of the temple:

The whole area surrounding the mountaintop is most holy.

Behold, this is the law of the temple."

Ezekiel 43:10-12

Chapter One

YAHWEH'S HOUSE

"And they said, 'Come, let us build ourselves a city, and a tower whose top is in the heavens; let us make a name for ourselves, lest we be scattered abroad over the face of the whole earth.' But the LORD came down to see the city and the tower which the sons of men had built. And the LORD said, 'Indeed the people are one and they all have one language, and this is what they begin to do; now nothing that they propose to do will be withheld from them.'" Genesis 11:4-9

For millennia, reaching back to the dawn of civilization, humanity has harbored the ambitious aspiration of bridging the vast chasm between mortal existence and the gods who dwell in the heavenly realms. Driven by an innate and often subconscious yearning for a profound spiritual connection with their Creator, humans have erected magnificent towers in a quest to establish contact and communion with the gods of these realms. In Mesopotamia, these towers were called ziggurats, the most famous of which was the Tower of Babel spoken of in the book of Genesis. God put an end to this project by confusing the language of the people and scattering their efforts to the four corners of the world.

From that time, and throughout history, to this present day, the drive to build high towers or tall buildings has remained ingrained in man's psyche. Competition amongst the industrial nations of the world as to who was superior architecturally, and the most technologically advanced, gave rise to the pursuit of becoming the nation to build the highest structure.

America gave us the Washington Monument built in 1848 at 555 ft; the cornerstone of this tower, designed after the Egyptian obelisk, was laid with elaborate Masonic ceremonies. France gave us the Eiffel Tower in 1889 at 984 ft. high. America went on to dominate in the building of tall structures with the twin towers of the World Trade Centre completed in 1970, at 1368 ft. and the Sears Tower built in 1974 at 1450 ft. The Petronas Tower in Kuala Lumpur then topped them all at 1483 ft. built in 1996. Toronto Canada achieved great status giving us the CN Tower, the world's tallest free-standing structure at 1,816 feet until more recently when Dubai built the Khalifa Tower at 2,717 feet.

The construction of tall towers or buildings is not only a reflection of man's spiritual longing, but it has also become a statement of power, status, and wealth. These tall towers that dominate the skyline of the cities of the world are the reflection of an idolatry that glorifies man and the world systems we live in. The Twin Towers of the World Trade Centre, representing the economic might of the United States, were reduced to rubble on September 11, 2001, by the enemies of America, and the enemies of the God of Abraham, Isaac, and Jacob. However, throughout Scripture, God has used and will continue to use the enemy as a rod of correction to remove and smash the idols standing between God and man.

The Bible reveals that God permitted the Babylonians to encroach upon His Land and take captive His people, as a form of discipline due to their unfaithfulness and idolatry. Throughout Scripture, we find accounts of God utilizing entities such as the Philistines, Babylonians, and Assyrians as instruments of discipline during periods when His people succumbed to idolatry (Isaiah 37:26-27).

"Truly, LORD, the kings of Assyria have laid waste all the nations and their lands, and have cast their gods into the fire; for they were not gods, but the work of men's hands—wood and stone. Therefore they destroyed them." Isaiah 37:18

The world is now reaping the consequence of placing its trust and security in world systems and its pantheon of gods, and not worshiping Yahweh, the one true and only God. Sadly, catastrophic events sometimes appear to inspire, even greater pride and arrogance in man, rather than the humility and repentance that is necessary to remove the sin at the root of such tragedies.

> *"When I shut up heaven and there is no rain, or command the locusts to devour the land, or send pestilence among My people, if My people who are called by My name will humble themselves, and pray and seek My face, and turn from their wicked ways, then I will hear from heaven, and will forgive their sin and heal their land."* 2 Chronicles 7:13-14

Many have shown that Canada and America were founded on Christian principles, yet our nations continue to daily trample the Son of God underfoot, insult the Spirit of grace, and count the precious Blood of Jesus as nothing, in pursuit of power and selfish aims inspired by a demonic agenda. Humanity has chosen to idolize the kingdoms of this world rather than the Kingdom of God and His Christ.

> *"Anyone who rejected the law of Moses died without mercy on the testimony of two or three witnesses. How much more severely do you think a man deserves to be punished who has trampled the Son of God underfoot, who has treated as an unholy thing the blood of the covenant that sanctified him, and who has insulted the Spirit of grace? For we know him who said, "It is mine to avenge; I will repay," and again, "The Lord will judge his people." It is a dreadful thing to fall into the hands of the living God."* Hebrews 10 28-31 NIV

Christian nations have grossly departed from the ways of God so brilliant and clear in the Person of Jesus Christ, and are choosing rather to embrace the character, nature, and ways of Satan. We cannot fight the enemy while embracing the nature of Satan. It is imperative for Christian nations today, to return to the ancient paths where the good way is.

"This is what the LORD says: "Stand at the crossroads and look; ask for the ancient paths, ask where the good way is, and walk in it, and you will find rest for your souls. But you said, 'We will not walk in it.' I appointed watchmen over you and said, "Listen to the sound of the trumpet!' But you said, 'We will not listen.' Therefore hear, O nations; observe, O witnesses, what will happen to them. Hear, O earth: I am bringing disaster on this people, the fruit of their schemes, because they have not listened to my words and have rejected my law." Jeremiah 6:16-19 NIV

Attempting to confront the spirit of anti-Christ within terrorist nations and organizations while harboring sin in our hearts and relying solely on worldly weapons is a recipe for certain defeat. No sooner have we destroyed one antichrist, ten more arise in its place—the last state is then worse than the first. The only weapon possessing the power to consistently overcome Satan is and has always been *the Cross of Jesus Christ.*

When Isaiah humbled himself in prayer, seeking divine intervention against the imminent Assyrian invasion, God's initial response was poignant: *"...because you have prayed"* (Isaiah 37:21). In times of divine judgment, whether through pestilence, drought, or demonic locusts, the singular prerequisite for God's attention and healing of the land is humility in prayer (2 Chronicles 7:14). The current shaking of the earth serves as a warning that, beyond Christ, there is no refuge from the wrath to come.

"He who dwells in the secret place of the Most High shall abide under the shadow of the Almighty." Psalm 91:1

The Almighty God, the One and only God of Heaven and Earth, has predetermined in His wisdom that the *only structure,* that will ever remove the veil, and close the gap between Heaven and Earth, is the Temple of *'The Christ.'* This magnificent edifice is the singular *Strong Tower* that attains to the exalted heights of

Heaven, touching the very Throne of a Holy God. God began to build this edifice, approximately four thousand years ago on the soil of Jerusalem, and He will complete it *in Jerusalem*, in the early part of the third millennium after Christ (the morning of the third day, John 2:19).

God laid the foundation of Yahweh's House in Christ before the foundation of the earth, as He is *"...the Lamb slain from the foundation of the Earth"* (Rev. 13:8). When He *"descended to the lower earthly regions..."* and *"...ascended higher than all the heavens..."* (Eph. 4:9-10) and *"...sat down at the right hand of the Majesty on high"* (Heb.1:3), He established its span!

Jesus, the Word, became flesh and dwelt (or was 'tabernacled') among us. *'The Christ'* became the living Temple of God, the soles of His feet and the place of His Throne secured in Jerusalem, Israel *forever*.

> *"And He said to me, "Son of man, this is the place of My throne and the place of the soles of My feet, where I will dwell amid the children of Israel forever." Ezekiel 43:7*

> *"The glory of Lebanon shall come to you, the cypress, the pine, and the box tree together, To beautify the place of My sanctuary; And I will make the place of My feet glorious." Isaiah 60:13*

This majestic tower of *'The Christ'* is epitomized by the towering majesty of Mount Zion, ascending into the heavens where the Throne of God reigns supreme. God Himself stands as the Architect of this Heavenly structure, and Jesus Christ, empowered by the Holy Spirit, serves as the Master Builder. He is the *only One* ordained to build this Temple in reverence to God the Father. He exclusively, through the agency of the Holy Spirit, orchestrates and oversees every facet of its construction. The builders chosen to participate in this transcendent endeavor are handpicked by Him, serving as vessels through whom the completion of this Divine Temple will be realized.

"Unless the Lord builds the house, they labor in vain who build it..." Psalm 127:1

The definition of the word 'edifice' is a *beautiful, extraordinary, or monumental building.* It is the root of the word 'edify,' which means to build up or to build upward. Within the construction of Yahweh's House, each believer serves as a living stone embedded with a divine calling to engage in the work of edification. Our collective effort is directed towards growing the Body of Christ, building upward to the very Throne of God, to Christ who is the Head (Ephesians 4:10-15).

At present, we find ourselves navigating the concluding stages of this spiritual construction, ascending the scaffolds of God's precepts, revelations, and vision as we diligently partner in this grand undertaking.

When Moses completed the building of the Tabernacle of God according to God's instructions, the Glory of the Lord filled the Tabernacle. After Solomon completed the building of the Temple of God according to the instructions his father David had received from God, the *Glory of the Lord filled the House of God* (1 Chron. 28:19). Isaiah, Ezekiel, Haggai, and John in the book of Revelation, were all given visions of a Temple at the end of the age, filled with the Glory of the Lord to such an extent that the entire earth was touched by its Glory.

"Thus says the Lord of hosts: 'Once more (it is a little while) I will shake heaven and earth, the sea and dry land; and I will shake all nations, and they shall come to the Desire of All Nations, and I will fill this temple with glory,' says the LORD of hosts...'The glory of this latter temple shall be greater than the former,' says the LORD of hosts. 'And in this place, I will give peace.' Says the LORD of hosts." Haggai 2:6

According to Scripture, the Lord begins this time of shaking at the *House of the Lord.* Everything that can be shaken, that does not have its source in the Heart and Mind of Christ must be shaken free of His Body. The Church and the world are about to pass through the Consuming Fire of God, as He draws close for judgment. We must allow the Lord to do the work of refinement in us now, so that we may be able to dwell in the devouring fire at the end of the age and not be burned up.

"The sinners in Zion are afraid; fearfulness has seized the hypocrites: "Who among us shall dwell with the devouring fire? Who among us shall dwell with everlasting burnings?" He who walks righteously and speaks uprightly, He who despises the gain of oppressions, who gestures with his hands, refusing bribes, who stops his ears from hearing of bloodshed, and shuts his eyes from seeing evil: He will dwell on high; His place of defense will be the fortress of rocks; Bread will be given him, His water will be sure." Isaiah 33:14

The Lord has presently begun the work of rebuilding His House—the House that will receive Christ at His return in all His Power and Glory. Yahweh's House will be characterized by Christ in His fullness of deity. Jesus *'The Christ'* is the House of God! Jesus Christ is the fulfillment of *the House of God* revealed to Jacob at Bethel. He is the Gate of Heaven, the Gate to eternal life.

"...and there the angels of God were ascending and descending on it..." How awesome is this place! This is none other than the house of God and this is the gate of heaven!" Genesis 28:12, 17

This House becomes the sacred Place where the angels of God ascend and descend. Within this Holy dwelling, God presides over an open heaven, revealing the profound connection between Heaven and Earth.

As the last days unfold, an unprecedented release of the angelic hosts will be witnessed. This is a Divine collaboration with the saints to diligently prepare the Headstone Sanctuary of Yahweh's House for the Return of the King.

27

"Most assuredly, I say to you, hereafter you shall see heaven open, and the angels of God ascending and descending upon the Son of Man." John 1:51

_____

_____

_____

_____

_____

_____

_____

Chapter Two

EZEKIEL'S TEMPLE

"In the visions of God He took me into the land of Israel and set me on a very high mountain; on it toward the south was something like the structure of a city. He took me there, and behold, there was a man whose appearance was like the appearance of bronze. He had a line of flax and a measuring rod in his hand, and he stood at the gateway." Ezekiel 40:2-3

Ezekiel's temple represents God's design of the temple that will house His Presence in the fullness of His Glory, for all eternity (ch.47:3). Chapter 40 is the line of demarcation between the old and a *new generation*, between the old dispensation marked by sin and rebellion, God's wrath and judgment, and a *new era* characterized by holiness, prepared for His eternal habitation.

The number forty in the Bible represents a generation, and also a period of profound refinement and testing. After a period of severe judgment described in the chapters leading up to chapter 40, chapter 39 ends with a prophetic picture of God's grace and mercy being poured out on His people. Out of this River of Mercy, the revelation of the beginning of something tremendous and new unfolds in chapters 40 through 48—*the blueprint symbolic of the end-time temple of the Lord.*

"And the man said to me, "Son of man, look with your eyes and hear with your ears, and fix your mind on everything I show you; for you were brought here so that I might show them to

you. Declare to the house of Israel everything you see." Ezekiel 40:4-5

Chapter 40 opens with a man whose appearance was like 'the appearance of bronze.' This man has a measuring rod in his hand and for the next eight chapters, he goes about measuring, measuring, and continually measuring, every detail of a City and a Temple representative of the last day Temple that is 'The Christ' in fullness—the City of God. At its completion, the name of the City is changed by God to *'Yahweh Shamah'* meaning *The LORD is There* (Ez. 48:35).

This *man of bronze* is representative of Christ, who makes His appearance throughout the Old Testament as the *'Angel of the Lord.'* The measurements given are symbolic of something more profound and much greater than a physical temple as they represent 'The Christ' in His fullness of Glory. Jesus is the Architect and Builder of His temple, the only One in possession of the measurements of His future eternal dwelling, as they are embedded within Him.

An outstanding feature of this Temple is that in every detail it is 'Most Holy' and because of this the River of God is released from the Throne to flow out as a healing River to the nations of the World (Ez.47). This Most Holy Temple is Christ in Glory—built on the Pattern of Christ. It represents *man in the fullness of union with God.*

> *"For this One has been counted worthy of more glory than Moses, inasmuch as He who built the house has more honor than the house. For every house is built by someone, but He who built all things is God." Hebrews 3:3*

This Temple cannot be built by man as it is Spiritual and God alone is its builder. The pattern is not of this world. Truths of far greater importance than numerical measurements are being imparted to Ezekiel that came directly from Heaven. The Pattern is

Christ! The Man of Bronze is meticulous about every detail as this Temple must represent Christ accurately in His fullness.

In His building work, God is on a continual movement forward. He is not returning to the past, to old ways that were only meant to serve as stepping stones toward the fullness of Life in His Presence. I do not believe that we will be returning to the rituals of animal sacrifices in the future, as the Lamb has been slain once and for all (Heb. 7:26).

"In that He says, A new covenant, He has made the first obsolete" (Heb. 8:13, 9:9-10, 10:8-14). The sacrifice of animals could never satisfy God or remove sin—Jesus alone holds that place of honor.

The Temple of God was built of stone in the natural but was transformed into a Spiritual Living Temple at the death and resurrection of Jesus Christ and by the entrance of the *Breath* of Life—the Holy Spirit.

"Sacrifice and offering You did not desire, but a body You have prepared for Me. In burnt offerings and sacrifices for sin You had no pleasure. Then I said, 'Behold, I have come—In the volume of the book it is written of Me—to do Your will, O God."
Hebrews 10: 5-7

The Spiritual Temple of God is *a body*, a temple built on sacrifice—the giving of one's life in service of another. Paul regarded himself as a drink offering poured out to God for His Glory. The sacrifices and offerings in the Temple of God are the lives of God's people offered in service to the nations of the world.

"I beseech you therefore, brethren, by the mercies of God, that you present your bodies a living sacrifice, holy, acceptable to God, which is your reasonable service." Romans 12:1

As we have progressed in Spiritual understanding over the centuries, a clearer and more accurate picture of this Temple has been coming closer into view. It is vital at this point in His story to build accurately and precisely according to the Heavenly Pattern. The need is to prepare the *Most Holy Place,* having the dynamics to house *the Christ* in the full weight of His Glory. This means cutting away at faulty perceptions based on carnal thinking and breaking down and eliminating old religious mindsets. It became necessary for Jesus to do this at His first coming and will again become necessary in preparation for His Second Coming!

God, the Father is preparing a people in union with Christ, to complete His will and finish the purposes of God on Earth (Heb. 10:5-7). This community of people from every tribe and nation is being built up into a dynamic Spiritual Temple constructed from the very Life of Christ. Every detail and measurement of this Temple has been established from Heaven before the foundations of the earth. Because it bears the image of Christ and is constructed with the very Life of Christ, as God fills it with His Glory—*the River of God is released from it in its fullness to flood the Earth!*

The Man of Bronze is now preparing the ground to build this last Temple, the Most Holy Place of Christ. This is the *last phase* of the building work of the one overall comprehensive Temple built over history. We have arrived at the time to prepare *the Headstone or final stone of the Temple.* At its Completion God will declare its new name over it—*Yahweh Shamah—Yahweh, He is there!*

Chapter Three

THE MOST HOLY PLACE

"The priests then brought the ark of the LORD'S covenant to its place in the inner sanctuary of the temple, the Most Holy Place, and put it beneath the wings of the cherubim." 1 Kings 8:6

To build the Temple that is *The Christ*, in the closing hour of this era, a precise revelation, combined with understanding and wisdom is required. Jesus is returning, and the Holy Spirit *will* prepare a resting place for the Ark of His Presence. The builders who build with the Holy Spirit will receive a paradigm shift in present mindsets, *as all realms and structures begin to shift into the new dynamic of the last day to accommodate the Presence of the coming King.* The pathway to His return is being made straight, representing a way we have not walked before!

> *"Prepare the way of the LORD; Make straight in the desert a highway for our God. Every valley shall be exalted and every mountain and hill brought low; the crooked places shall be made straight and the rough places smooth; the glory of the LORD shall be revealed..." Isaiah 40:3-5*

The first illusion to be eliminated in carnal patterns is the *perception of separation* existing on a subliminal level between the Body of Christ, and *Christ the Head.* Having this perception, that we are here on Earth and God is separated from us, in some far away place, gives place to complacency regarding sin. This false perception comes from an ungodly belief residing below the threshold of consciousness of the Body of Christ. It is an ungodly belief that has created an environment conducive to disobedience, a lack of accountability to a Holy and Awesome God, and a diminishing measure of the *fear of the Lord*. It strongly influences what is permitted in our personal lives, our bodies, and within the broader Body of Christ. This deceptive *perception of separation* encourages a sense of liberty to act independently of God, apart from submission to His Word—without suffering any consequences.

I believe that this perception has been allowed to exist *to motivate the passionate heart to pursue God*, to become complete in Him in the union of mind, heart, and soul. It is removed with maturity and conformity to Christ. It is ultimately eliminated as Christ is formed in the believer, and *there is growth toward the Head to the stature of Christ* where there is completion and union in Him (Col. 2:19, Eph. 4:15, Gal. 4:19).

> *"They have lost connection with the head, from whom the whole body, supported and held together by its ligaments and sinews, grows as God causes it to grow." Colossians 2:19*

In a walk characterized by rebellion and pride, the lukewarm heart comes under a contrasting effect: the gap of separation widens, pulling the individual away from a Christ-centric dynamic. The enemy is then given room to impede spiritual growth and hamper progress toward maturity. On such a path, sensitivity to the Lord is diminished, discernment gets distorted, and understanding of God's intentions within and through His people gets obscured.

For full union to take place and the gap closed, there must be the recognition *through revelation*, that the Body of Christ *is Christ's Body* and is a *Most Holy Place*. From the soles of His feet to His Head, the place of the Throne—*He is the Temple of God*. He is *one* being that is *both* Head and Body. When Christ is received at salvation, we are planted by God into *His very* being. We become a part of Him and have our being in Him. Our lives are then caught up in the momentum of His Destiny and are progressively consumed in the fire of His Holy Presence. Holding this perspective is exceedingly crucial to maturity.

"Do you not know that your bodies are members of Christ? Shall I then take the members of Christ and make them members of a harlot?" 1 Corinthians 6:15

When this transcendent revelation is apprehended, that believers have been planted *into* the Holy Place of *Christ's Body*, attitudes will change dramatically, producing an embrace of *the fear of the Lord* and a delight to do His will!

Born-again Christians have become embedded within an all-consuming God. Their lives have become caught up in the awesome momentum of *Divine flow,* moving with supernatural power and force toward the fulfillment of *Christ's* Destiny. His face and His Life have been fixed and directed toward a specific goal from the foundations of the earth—to rule and to reign over the kingdoms of this world with His Bride at His side ruling with Him.

Jesus is on the move toward a destination, and if you belong to Him, and if you are a part of *His* Body, you are moving in the powerful current of His Life, caught up in the momentum of *His Passion.*

"For He rescued us from darkness and brought us into the kingdom of the Son He loves." Colossians 2:3

"And you know that He was manifested to take away our sins, and in Him there is no sin. Whoever abides in Him does not sin. Whoever sins has neither seen Him nor known Him. Little children, let no one deceive you. He who practices righteousness is righteous, just as He is righteous. He who sins is of the devil, for the devil has sinned from the beginning. For this purpose the Son of God was manifested, that He might destroy the works of the devil." 1 John 3:5-8

35

As Christians, we reside in the *Most Holy Place* of Christ, in His Body. At our salvation, God bought the whole package with His Blood. But although we were then planted into this *Holy Place,* the fullness of Christ did not necessarily take full possession of the soul at that time. The soul before salvation can be likened to a piece of property or land occupied and owned by the enemy, in enemy territory. At salvation, Christ purchases the land with His Blood. The Holy Spirit then establishes a beachhead in the land. With the believer fully surrendered to His will, He moves out from this position. Ground is gained in the soul, as the ability to drive out the enemy and occupy and hold the ground He has won is acquired. When continuing to work with Him in this process, His Presence moves out to occupy and permeate the entire land, drawing everything into the Lord's Mind and Will.

The measure of Christ's Life received and processed at salvation can be quite fragile in comparison to the fullness of Christ that is attained with persistence. The enemy plans to overwhelm and strangle the new Life of Christ where there is no strong foundation, where there is a lack of understanding of the ways and Word of God, and because of the worries of life and the deceitfulness of wealth (Matt. 13:18-23). The new Life of Christ in the heart must be nurtured sufficiently, fed daily, and cared for passionately if it is to grow in knowledge and understanding to the measure of the stature of His fullness—to a complete Man, *"...until Christ is formed in you"* (Gal.4:19).

The places in us that continue to remain in rebellion act as mutant cells in the Body working against it and the greater Body of Christ—a *disease that must and will be eradicated by the cleansing agent of the Blood through repentance.* This can reflect a picture of the condition of the soul, local churches, and the global Church in the macro view. God owns it all and has established beachheads and strongholds of His Presence in every nation, through local community churches and gatherings—*His Life continually increasing until He occupies the whole.*

Statistics on religions place Christianity in 2022 at approximately thirty-one percent of the world's population. If Christ is the Temple of the *Most Holy Place*, then a large portion of the Church is living in the Outer Court—the outer layer of the Body representing flesh and carnality.

When the revelation of our place in the Body and Temple of Christ is received, saints will begin to live from that vision with fresh consecration and purpose. The Body is becoming built together into the Most Holy Temple of *The Christ*. God's endgame is our arrival at the Place of holy union: *"...to a perfect man, to the measure of the stature of the fullness of Christ..."* (Eph. 4:11-13).

> *"For as the body is one and has many members, but all the members of that one body, being many, are one body, so also is Christ. For by one Spirit we were all baptized into one body..."* 1Corinthians 12:13

The entirety of what is essential for the believer's deliverance was secured through Jesus' triumph on the Cross. However, sanctification is a process accomplished *over time.* While God can grant us full deliverance on the day of salvation, in practice, this doesn't usually occur. He uses the process of deliverance to progressively build His Life and nature into the believer as the maturity to occupy and hold the ground He intends to give is acquired.

> *"I will not drive them out from before you in one year, Lest the land become desolate and the beast of the field become too numerous for you. Little by little I will drive them out from before you, until you have increased, and you inherit the land."* Exodus 23:29-30

To experience the increase of the Lord's Presence and Life in the land of the soul, the believer is encouraged to willingly decrease by surrendering all aspects of their lives to Him for cleansing and deliverance. As desires are relinquished and wills are submitted, the Holy Spirit's influence expands, as all things become consumed and conformed to God's Will. When wholeheartedly embraced, this process leads to a profound union with the Lord, complete immersion into His Life, and overflowing fullness where the self-life becomes crucified.

> *"I have been crucified with Christ; it is no longer I who live, but Christ lives in me; and the life which I now live in the flesh I live by faith in the Son of God, who loved me and gave Himself for me." Galatians 2:20*

The places of rebellion and intentional sin within believers, not filled by the Holy Spirit and occupied by Christ cannot belong to *the Holy Place of His Body*. These areas of rebellion that some stubbornly cling to—areas tainted by gross sin, division, worldly agendas, or lifeless religious practices, remain outside of the sanctified sphere of His holiness. The ongoing integration of the Church into the Lord's Divine Life occurs through the continuous baptism into His Life. The expected end is *full union*. In the end, everything not found in Him—all sin and works of the flesh, are ultimately burned up in the Fire of His Holiness.

> *"If anyone's work is burned, he will suffer loss; but he himself will be saved, yet so as through fire. Do you not know that you are the temple of God and that the Spirit of God dwells in you? ...If anyone defiles the temple of God, God will destroy him. For the temple of God is holy, which temple you are. Let no one deceive himself. If anyone among you seems to be wise in this age, let him become a fool that he may become wise." 1Corinthians 3:17*

The *Body of Christ* as *a Most Holy place* cannot be joined with *intentional sin*, and given sufficient time to repent, will reject rebellion, sin, witchcraft, and disobedience. In the last days, every knee will bow.

> *"Not everyone who says to Me, 'Lord, Lord,' shall enter the kingdom of heaven, but he who does the will of My Father in heaven. Many will say to Me in that day, 'Lord, Lord, have we*

not prophesied in Your name, cast out demons in Your name, and done many wonders in Your name?' And then I will declare to them, 'I never knew you; depart from Me, you who practice lawlessness!' Matthew 7:21-23

The Blood of Jesus does not cover *intentional disobedience and rebellion*, such sin will fall under judgment. Only through true repentance, the *turning away and rejection of sin*, moved by Godly fear and sorrow, does the Blood cleanse these sinful areas and consume them as if they never were.

God intended that life in Christ be defined by the journey of ascension, in a continual movement from *Glory to Glory* as it grows up into the stature of Christ, the Head. Jesus said, *"I am the resurrection and the Life."* The process of Jesus being reproduced in the life of the believer as it is integrated into the Divine Life of Christ is Holy and eternal.

"See that you do not refuse Him who speaks. For if they did not escape who refused Him who spoke on earth, much more shall we not escape if we turn away from Him who speaks from heaven, whose voice then shook the earth; but now He has promised, saying, "YET ONCE MORE I SHAKE NOT ONLY THE EARTH, BUT ALSO HEAVEN." Now this, "YET ONCE MORE," indicates the removal of those things that are being shaken, as of things that are made, that the things which cannot be shaken may remain. Therefore, since we are receiving a kingdom which cannot be shaken, let us have grace, by which we may serve God acceptably with reverence and godly fear. For our God is a consuming fire." Hebrews 12:25-29

The forces of death cannot imprison the Life of Christ in the Body, but they will try. What is not of Christ in it will continually seek to work against the corporate *Body of Christ* to imprison the Life and the Light of Christ from coming forth.

Jesus Christ is the *'Most Holy Place,'* encased in a tomb of religion and religious dead works. He is presently moving to *break and shake Himself free* as all things Holy and eternal are *summed up and completed in Him.* Only that which is found *in Him* is eternal and remains!

The Lord will use His mighty *Sword of Truth* to slice through all deceptions, dividing soul from spirit, bone from marrow, and the Holy from the carnal. He is peeling away the carnal flesh of the Outer Court and cutting through the smallest deceptions that continue to cling to His Body, create mixture, and distort the Truth of God. Believers have been given the choice of whether to go through this process with Him. In the end, it must be found that *He is all, and fills all*, as He shapes and works to integrate each of us as vibrant radiant, healthy cells in *His Body characterized by the Divine!*

The manifest Presence of the Almighty God of Heaven and Earth, represented by the Ark of the Lord's covenant, resides in the *Most Holy Place* of the Temple—not in the Outer Court or even in the Holy Place. God is Holy and His Presence dwells in Holiness. *This place is where we dwell in union with Him.* It is a place where flesh cannot survive, and all iniquity is consumed.

The Holy of Holies also called the *Most Holy Place, is the habitation of God.* The completing phase of the Temple of His Body is being prepared as the *Most Holy Place* for His return. As the veil was torn at the Cross, the way into the *Most Holy Place* was opened. God is giving those who choose to live in the outer Court time to press into the safety of His Presence.

The Altar of incense was positioned in the temple in the *Most Holy Place* before the Lord. This portrays the closeness of our communion with God through prayer.

"Behind the second curtain was a room called the Most Holy Place, which had the golden altar of incense and the gold covered ark of the covenant." Hebrews 8:3 NIV

In the book of Revelation, all sixteen references to *the finished temple* are the Greek word *naos* which according to Strong's Concordance, denotes the central sanctuary that is the *Most Holy Place* as opposed to *hieron* which denotes the larger precinct. This reveals that the Temple of the Last Days will be the Sanctuary of God's *Most Holy Place*.

> *"Rise and measure the temple of God, the altar, and those who worship there. But leave out the court which is outside the temple, and do not measure it, for it has been given to the Gentiles. And they will tread the holy city underfoot for forty-two months." Revelation 11:1-2*

_____

_____

_____

_____

_____

_____

_____

Chapter Four

JOURNEY INTO THE HOLY OF HOLIES

"For thus says the High and Lofty One who inhabits eternity, whose name is Holy: "I dwell in the high and holy place, with him who has a contrite and humble spirit, to revive the spirit of the humble, And to revive the heart of the contrite ones." Isaiah 57:15

To build for Himself a Holy Habitation, God set apart a specific portion of Land as the building site. In scripture, He referred to this Land as *His portion*. It became known as the Holy Land because it was the clay with which the Master Potter would shape the Man having the Face and countenance of Yahweh. The prophets and apostles of Israel became the voices God used to deliver the architectural Blueprint of His house modeled after this Man and the nation became the construction *worksite*.

The wall constructed around this sacred site became the Will of God as transcribed by the prophets in the Word of God. The power inherent in God's Word ensured the ongoing work moved forward and that the builders were unhindered as the majestic structure rose over History.

When the nation took their eyes off God—the Lawgiver—and became enamored and consumed with matters of law—the law became an idol to them. The *law* of Judaism and a portion of *the wall* of the temple are all that remains of God for most Jewish people today. However, the Spiritual Temple of *Jeshua Messiah* continues to rise, ascending to the Throne and will meet Him in the air upon His return.

In the initial phase of a believer's spiritual journey, as He does with the Holy Land, the Holy Spirit builds the scaffold of God's Word around the construction site of the new life to shield and protect His work. This is fundamental as the scriptures serve to build the principles of God, needed for empowerment and growth in the Life of Christ. God's Word reveals and exposes the nature of sin, providing the understanding that service is to a Holy God. It underscores the necessity of obedience to maintaining a relationship with God. It makes ready the heart to yield to the Father's will through the Holy Spirit's work.

FREEDOM IN CHRIST

"For Christ is the end of the law for righteousness to everyone who believes." Romans 10:4

The law is no longer a measurement of righteousness in the people of God. Christ who fulfilled the law, and by His sacrifice for sin, has put an end to that system and the religious spirit. The word *'end'* in this scripture is the word *telos*, which means; *to set out for a definite point or goal; the point aimed at as a limit; the conclusion.* The journey of one called to leadership, continues over a lifetime in a movement on the ascent to fullness in Christ, leading it to life in the fiery Presence of God in the *Holy of Holies. Life in the Spirit* concludes with *union in Christ.*

With growth and maturity toward Christlikeness and life lived in the *Holy of Holies,* the need for formulas, regulations, and patterns is eradicated, as Christ is the Formula and Pattern the House is being *conformed to.* The pinnacle of the mountain is union with Christ—a journey completed *by His grace alone.*

The wall of Fire that surrounds and guards the Temple of *The Christ* is the reflection of the radiance of His Presence and

Holiness. By their proximity to Him, His character and ways become seared into the hearts of emerging apostolic leadership.

It was never God's intent for His priesthood to settle down at the law as Israel's did. Law and order are the prepared ground for discipline, learning, and the acquiring of spiritual knowledge and understanding. This is now written on the heart of God's priesthood. From this place of a submitted heart, the Holy Spirit, who cannot work outside of *God's order,* then moves His consecrated ones onto the higher plane of *Life in the Spirit.*

God's Apostolic/prophetic leaders are led by and called to obey the Holy Spirit—*the One sent as the guardian and administrator of the Word of God.* This may appear to be a simplistic statement but has proven to not always be the case in terms of leadership in the House of God. In the example set by Christ, He shows it is a walk of faith in union with Him, where judgment is by the Spirit, not by what is seen or heard (Is. 11:3).

God may choose to begin His work in a church, or ministry in a way characterized by *law and order*—with strong teaching and discipline, to lay the firm foundation of His Word. When there is no growth or movement beyond this place, the Word can become an idol and eventually a prison, where the liberty of Life in the Spirit is lost. Similar to the Pharisees' fall, the tendency to idolize the written Word creeps in, rather than engagement in the worship of the Living Word—Jesus Christ.

God may also choose to begin *a work* in the power of the Spirit, with signs and wonders, and revelation of the possibility of life in the Spirit outside of legalism. The wine breaks out and all chaos ensues. It may be Holy chaos and wonderful. However, if the Spirit-led groundwork of sound teaching, marked by humility, and submission to the Word of God and the protocols of God, is not established by leaders *who have this foundation in themselves,* chaos can ensue that can give place to the demonic. Foundations and balance are the key—both the Word and the Spirit are needed!

All the precepts and counsels of the Word of God must be taught and embedded in His House, not just a preferred few that leaders are comfortable with. On the journey with God, if we take our eyes off Him to remain and gaze at any of the wonderful gifts He gives, these places will eventually become places of idolatry or roadblocks on the climb toward the pinnacle of Glory in Christ.

"For as many as are led by the Spirit of God, these are the sons of God." Romans 8:14

The Outer Court of the Temple symbolizes the realm of lukewarm religion and commercialized practices. However, with perseverance, and by the Grace of God, the soul hungry for God will transition from Outer Court living to life in the Holy Place. The arduous journey through the maze of religious doctrines, fueled by a sincere longing to know and serve God, becomes the training ground where foundations are built in His leaders. Here, the ability to discern truth from deception is developed, and Saints are equipped to live in alignment with the Holy Spirit.

"I give thanks to Him who has granted me [the needed] strength and made me able [for this]; Christ Jesus our Lord, because He has judged and counted me faithful and trustworthy appointing me to [this stewardship of] the ministry." 1 Timothy 1:12 AMP

With the choice to press on toward the *Holy Place* and embrace a life of service to God, saints become a priesthood who serve God's will and purposes. However, the Holy place can also become a place of works, legalistic religion, and much religious activity. There was much ecclesiastical work to be done by the priests in the Holy place, illustrating that even though leaders may be pressing on to draw closer to the Presence of God, much of what may consume their time can be merely a product of routine behavior void of the Presence of God.

The Holy Place may also be a place where leadership may be inclined to settle down and close their hearts from desiring to pursue more of God. Here, minds can become closed to the possibility of there being anything more, or a leader may develop the attitude of: *"The road to get here was long and rough and now I have finally arrived, I'll just rest in this Holy Place and fulfill my duties as God's minister."*

JOURNEY INTO THE HOLY OF HOLIES

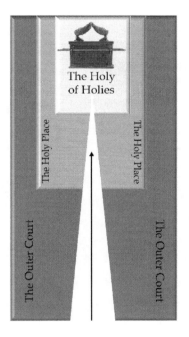

The Holy Place was never meant to be a place in which to simply work out our days or to settle down. *It was meant to serve as a bridge into the Holy of Holies.* It is a bridge that we burn behind us. Throughout history, God has been working to lead His people on a trajectory into life in the Spirit, away from the realms of law, religion, and works. Arrival in the *Holy of Holies* comes through great patience and perseverance in the many trials and tests—*the crucible that works to produce passionate apostolic leaders.* Here in this Place, *life and joy in His Presence are attained(Acts 2:25).* By proximity to Him, His leaders are continually being *fired* into His likeness.

We have now reached a pivotal juncture in history where the imperative is to construct the Divine last-day Temple of God—*the Holy of Holies*. It is within this sacred place that we are destined to reside, eternally connected with Almighty God in the radiant blaze of His Holy Presence.

This last-day Temple blueprinted in Heaven is currently undergoing a profound transformation, as it breaks free and sheds its Outer Court skin. It will ascend in Resurrection Glory, poised to unite with the returning Christ. The Holy of Holies, the abode of God, is beckoning, calling for all to come in. For those whose hearts blaze with fervent passion for God, this is His chosen place of residence. Despite the intense fire to get there, they willingly pay the price.

Many churches and ministries may be convinced of the measurements they use for building God's House, each employing Scripture as their basis for argument and debate. However, on the journey toward this sacred destination, the realization dawns that God alone by His Spirit constructs the Sanctuary of the Holy of Holies—*His divine and eternal dwelling place.* He alone has the measurements. Within this sacred space, works of the flesh do not survive as Jesus is the measure. From this innermost Sanctuary, the life force of Jesus emanates, pulling everything into the embrace of His Holy Fire.

"Who among us shall dwell with the devouring fire? Who among us shall dwell with everlasting burnings?" Isaiah 33:14

I once heard the Lord say: *"Denominations are points of settlements along the Journey on the ascent to Christ."* The Body of Christ is on a journey ascending toward a Divine appointment with Yahweh God in *the Holy of Holies.* Encampments along the Journey are places where His people have either settled in the complacency of the *Outer court* or the religion of *the Holy Place.* These are places where leaders have settled and camped on certain truths or doctrines and made idols of them.

Jesus is the Pinnacle of Mt. Zion. He is the Way and He is the Truth. Like our universe, when intentionally explored, truth is forever expanding, gaining depth, height, and width in the expanse and the surpassing greatness of His being.

There is no end to Christ! No boundaries can contain Him! No walls can hold Him! Should the mistake be made of becoming fixed in a position, Spiritual Life declines and becomes *organized and devoid of the Spirit*. Whatever we do have, will then be *"taken away"* (Matt. 13:12). Denominations, regulations, rituals, doctrines, and laws all belong in the *Outer Court* or *the Holy Place*. In *the Holy of Holies* all that there is, and all that is ever needed, is Yahweh—the Self-Existent eternal God. *Yahweh Shamah, GOD is there!*

The Body is being conformed and *fired* into the image and measurement of *a Person*—Christ Jesus. It is easy to forget this and get caught up in carnal legalistic measurements for the building of this Holy Temple.

To confidently advance and meticulously prepare this Holy Sanctuary for His return, it is crucial to now reflect on the early stages of the journey and assess the current position. We can then discern the guidance the Lord is providing at this juncture to move us forward on our ascent in Him.

The upcoming section will examine the Blueprint and constitution of the House of God, He is restoring, to return it to His original intentions. We will delve into the multifaceted phases in the construction of this sacred edifice and also explore the diverse models God has employed over the passage of time to fashion for Himself a Holy eternal Dwelling place. Our exploration will trace these models from the foundational inception of The House to the fullness of the Blueprint poised for realization in the culmination of time.

THE CONSTITUTION
& BLUEPRINT
OF THE HOUSE OF GOD

"For he was looking forward

To the city with foundations,

Whose architect and

builder *is God.*"

Hebrews 11:10 NIV

Chapter Five

THE ALTAR OF GOD

God is now moving to restore His House to the pattern it was first founded on—the House birthed in His Son Jesus. In building the House of God, the first and foremost element to be established is the Altar. This piece of furnishing is patterned after the Cross and represents sacrifice. It represents God's sovereignty and epitomizes His heart for a House of Prayer for all nations. This is the model now being restored for the *last days* and Christ's future reign on Earth.

The first mention of the Altar is in the book of Genesis where Noah offered a sacrifice that was a pleasing aroma to God. Because of this offering, the course of history was changed, revealing the power of the Altar and of sacrifice.

> *"Then Noah built an altar to the LORD and, taking some of all the clean animals and clean birds, he sacrificed burnt offerings on it. The LORD smelled the pleasing aroma and said in his heart: "Never again will I curse the ground because of humans, even though every inclination of the human heart is evil from childhood. And never again will I destroy all living creatures, as I have done." Genesis. 8:20*

After leaving the captivity of Babylon to rebuild the House of God, the Altar was the very first thing the returning captives sought to restore. They fully understood that the Altar had to be re-established to reconnect their relationship and submission to Yahweh God. They recognized they had no chance of survival without God's favor and providence over them. They knew that only by establishing the Altar to God that protection from the surrounding enemy nations would be provided.

"And they set the altar upon its bases; for fear was upon them because of the people of those countries: and they offered burnt offerings thereon unto the LORD, even burnt offerings morning and evening." Ezra 3:3 KJV

Verse six shows that they wisely built the Altar before the foundation of the House was even laid. This is important to note as the Altar of God is the central piece in God's House, linking all administrations of God in heaven and on Earth. Its supernatural significance is sublime by its very connection with the Throne of God in Heaven. To understand the power inherent in the Altar, we must first understand its implications and significance to God, and the protocols that surround it. The first and most important thing to note, that should inspire our awe, is that the Altar belongs to Yahweh God.

"Even them I will bring to My holy mountain, And make them joyful in My house of prayer. Their burnt offerings and their sacrifices Will be accepted on My altar; For My house shall be called a house of prayer for all nations." Isaiah 56:7

In man's approach to God at His Altar, there are protocols to be understood, as many have become compromised by sin. Christians today have not only allowed sin in their lives, but many also even entertain and relish in blatant sin and rebellion. God has not changed His mind about the consequences of defiling His Altar. The Word tells us that there no longer remains a sacrifice for sin for those who choose to sin willfully, who count the precious Blood of Jesus as a common thing (see Heb. 10:26-29).

"You have shown contempt by offering defiled sacrifices on My altar. "Then you ask, 'How have we defiled the sacrifices?' "You defile them by saying the altar of the LORD deserves no respect." Malachi 1:7

If our desire is to see the power of God break into this realm to bring transformation, we cannot afford to be people who say they fear the Lord, yet serve other gods. Humility and the fear of the Lord are the characteristics God is now looking for in the hearts of His servants. David fully understood God's heart's desire for purity, the reason God referred to him as a man after His own heart.

A psalm of David: "Who may worship in your sanctuary, LORD? Who may enter Your Presence on Your holy hill? He who walks uprightly, and works righteousness, and speaks the truth in his heart..." Psalm 15:1

A psalm of David: "Who may climb the mountain of the LORD? Who may stand in His holy place? He who has clean hands and a pure heart, Who has not lifted up his soul to an idol, Nor sworn deceitfully." Psalm 24:3-4

THE ALTAR OF SACRIFICE

David feared the Lord and when he sinned against the Lord by numbering his army, he cried out to God for mercy for his people. He then obediently followed the prophet Gad's instructions to build an Altar to the Lord.

"I have come to buy your threshing floor and to build an altar to the Lord there so that he will stop the plague."... I insist on buying it, for I will not present burnt offerings to the LORD my God that have cost me nothing." 2 Samuel 24:21,24 NLT

"David built an altar there to the LORD and sacrificed burnt offerings and peace offerings. And when David prayed, the LORD answered him by sending fire from heaven to burn up the offering on the altar. Then the LORD spoke to the angel, who put the sword back into its sheath." 1 Chronicles 21:26

There are many important points to understand from these passages: first, David acknowledged his sin and God's sovereignty over his life and the situation; he humbled himself and repented.

In obedience, he built an Altar to the Lord for a sacrificial offering. And lastly, he paid for the location having understood the Divine principle that the sacrifice must cost! After all protocols were adhered to, the plague was stopped! This very Altar became a very important one in God's unfolding and transcendent plan; it became not only the location for building the Temple of God but also the place allocated for the people of Israel to bring their offerings.

> *"Then David said, "This will be the location for the temple of the Lord God and the place of the altar for Israel's burnt offerings!" 1 Chronicles 22:1*

The Altar is the meeting place between the natural and the Divine, the place where the sacrificial offerings of the priests were supernaturally transported from the visible to the invisible, to the Throne of God in Heaven.

As God's appointed Sacrificial Lamb, the life of Christ defines the Altar! Jesus is the Altar of God! With His own Blood, Christ entered the Holy Place once and for all. He became the sacrifice once and for all time and all humanity (Heb. 9:11-28). Believers now approach this Altar by the Blood of Jesus! We have been invited to approach the Throne of God by Christ's shed Blood! In our repentance before God, saints acknowledge the costly sacrifice of Christ's life to appropriate forgiveness. A portal in Christ is now open for all at the Altar of God for the repentant soul!

THE ALTAR OF INCENSE

Moses was instructed to build a second Altar that represented communion with God—*the Altar of incense.* In the Old Testament, this Altar was set *before* the veil of the Holy of Holies. Behind the veil, the Ark of Testimony sat, where God would meet with the high priest. Once a year Aaron was instructed to take the blood of the sacrifice of the *sin offering* and place it on the horns of the Altar of Incense (Exodus 30:6-10).

This *Golden Altar* now sits *in front of* the Throne of God in Heaven. The Life, Presence, and intercession of Jesus are now the incense mingled and offered with the prayers of the saints!

> *"Another angel, who had a golden censer, came and stood at the altar. He was given much incense to offer, with the prayers of all God's people, on the golden altar in front of the throne. The smoke of the incense, together with the prayers of God's people, went up before God from the angel's hand. Then the angel took the censer, filled it with fire from the altar, and hurled it on the earth..." Revelation 8:3*

Remember when David built an altar and prayed, the LORD answered him also by sending *fire from heaven* to earth that burned up the offering. In this instance, the angel filled *the bowl of prayers* with Fire from the Altar and hurled it on the earth! Prayers that please God aligned with His will, release Fire!

As God continued to unveil revelations of His Altar, I began to sense the great activity in Heaven that surrounds it. The golden Altar was the Hub of Heaven around which Divine transactions founded on the intercession of God's people were taking place before the Presence of God. The Four Horns of the Altar anointed with Blood, represent the fullness of the Power of God in Christ. Jesus represents the Altar, the Power, the Fire and His is the Voice coming from is Horns of Power!

> *"The sixth angel sounded his trumpet, and I heard a voice coming from the four horns of the golden altar that is before God." Revelation 9:13*

The Altar depicts the utter Lordship of Christ over all affairs concerning God's people. On Earth, it is the place from which the fire of continual worship and prayer from a broken priesthood ascends before the Throne of God. It is the place where we meet with God, where important Kingdom business is enacted. Maintenance of an intimate and consequential relationship with God requires that hearts are purified and free of all idolatry.

The Altar is important to God because He desires that sacrificial, devotional offerings be offered continually to Him in worship—*costly offerings!* It cost Mary. It cost Paul. It cost Isaiah. It cost Jeremiah. The trajectory of history and a person's life can be forever changed by one sacrifice—*one costly offering,* as we see in the life of Abraham.

> *"Then I was given a reed like a measuring rod. And the angel stood, saying, "Rise and measure the temple of God, the altar, and those who worship there." Revelation 11:1*

The angel's command to measure the Altar and those who worshipped there shows its supreme significance to God. The Altar is the place of covenant, agreement, and security—it is, therefore, the first thing to be established as a representation of our agreement with Heaven. The Altar ultimately represents the binding relationship between God and man, rooted in a wholehearted commitment that calls for faithfulness and complete obedience to the will of God.

The Altar is the key to the power and fire of God being released to affect change. Intentionality about pursuing God in truth, beauty, holiness, and righteousness, is the Altar upon which the Fire falls, reflected in the heart of David.

> *"In that day the LORD will defend the inhabitants of Jerusalem; the one who is feeble among them in that day shall be like David, and the house of David shall be like God, like the Angel of the LORD before them. It shall be in that day that I will seek to destroy all the nations that come against Jerusalem." Zechariah 12:8-9*

These Davidic servants, builders of the House of God are being prepared to be invested with full authority, possessing full power, to transact business and execute judgments on behalf of the Kingdom of God. They have authorization to act on behalf of the Kingdom. These Leaders in God's Kingdom and of nations modeled after David are now being released to take their place in the heart of God. They live at the Altar and their lives have become living sacrifices. God will use them to implement His end-game strategies for the Kingdom. Apostolic men and women prepared for the last days, understand this.

In our service to the King, the first thing that must be instituted at the Altar is the contract of agreement with Him, ratified in the Blood of Jesus. Agreement is key to the power of God being released to affect change. Establishing the Altar is both urgent and strategic at this hour, as it opens the portal allowing for the councils on earth to meet with God to enact His will on Earth. God is presently moving to establish His Altar in houses where He is given His place as LORD. He is securing these places where the Holy Spirit is given full control.

The Altar is an inception point from where Heaven and Earth meet to work together to occupy and safeguard territory for the Kingdom of God! Once the portal is open and Heaven secures a beachhead and marks off the perimeter, the evidence of Christ's Lordship can be secured and established in that place! Apostolic leaders are being called to partner with the Holy Spirit and the Angel Armies to legislate the heavens, to align with God's purposes and will.

God is now calling to His leaders to leave spiritual Babylon and return to build the House of God it was founded on. He has opened the portal at His Altar in Christ where we meet with Him to conduct Kingdom affairs. He is now trumpeting the message, across the Earth:

Build Me an Altar! Build My Altar on Earth and take your place before Me!" Connect with the portal in Christ that I have opened for this Era. Here My Voice and receive power and strength from My Horns to fulfill your assignment.

Chapter Six

ISRAEL OR ROME?

The House of God, greatly impacted by Roman and Babylonian influences for over seventeen hundred years, will be restored to its pristine condition designed in the heart of God. With an understanding of the protocols and the constitution for building this House that will Host *Yahweh God,* it then becomes clear that all defiling, corrupting influences and mixture must be removed.

The Word of God given to humanity consists of God's messages and commands, that with adherence to its instructions, we may not be destroyed. These Divine instructions outlining the protocols for living in the presence of a Holy God comprise the whole counsel of God. There is nothing He has not taken into account and made provision for building His House.

With the establishment of *God's Altar* to a place of honor, representing submission and surrender, the restoration of *His Feasts* will follow. To understand the relationship and significance of the Feasts of God to the work of building the House of God, their *appointed times,* embedded in God's comprehensive time to get the job done, must be understood. To do so, we begin with the signs in the heavens given to mark time.

With His surpassing wisdom and unfathomable precision, God gave us the sun, the moon, and the stars as signs to serve in His Divine calendar to mark our times and the special Feast days appointed for His purposes. God ordained the *New Moon* as the herald of the advent of each month, marking transitions in Divine cycles that govern time.

> *"Then God said, "Let there be lights in the firmament of the heavens to divide the day from the night; and let them be for signs and seasons, and for days and years..." Genesis 1:14*

The Hebrew word *Chodesh* is the word used for the *new moon* and is also the word used for *month.* God commanded that on the day of the *new moon—on Rosh Chodesh—head of the month,* offerings were to be brought before Him in acts of worship. This ordinance is shown in scripture to continue into Jesus' millennial reign.

> *"For as the new heavens and the new earth Which I will make shall remain before Me," says the LORD, "So shall your descendants and your name remain. And it shall come to pass That from one New Moon to another, And from one Sabbath to another, All flesh shall come to worship before Me," says the LORD." Isaiah 66:22-23 (see also Zech. 14:16)*

The Feasts of God also marked the appointed times on God's calendar for the beginning and completion of His transcendent Plan of Redemption. The Hebrew word *moedim* means *appointed times* and is the word used in reference to the appointed times of God's Feasts. It is also the word sometimes used for *the congregation*—a revelation that the *Feasts of Yahweh* were significant appointments with God where *the congregation* gathered before Him bringing offerings of worship.

> *"Behold, I am building a temple for the name of the LORD my God, to dedicate it to Him, to burn before Him sweet incense, for the continual showbread, for the burnt offerings morning and evening, on the Sabbaths, on the New Moons, and on the set feasts of the LORD our God. This is an ordinance forever to Israel." 2 Chronicles 2:4*

The Biblical Feasts are ordained by God for *His people*—this includes the Gentiles who have been grafted into *the Israel of God.* The Feasts are not Jewish Feasts, as many say, they are *the Feasts of Yahweh,* transcending religion, and all religious practices. They are extremely significant and important to God as all Feasts represent His purposes as fulfilled in His Son Jesus on the specific dates set by Him! They represent intimate dreams dear to God's heart, each a prophetic fulfillment of the purposes of God in Christ. The Feasts are representative of God's calendar of events, each marking a milestone in His unfolding and transcendent Plan completed in Christ at His return.

> *"Speak to the children of Israel, and say to them: 'The feasts of the LORD, which you shall proclaim to be holy convocations, these are My feasts... 'These are the feasts of the LORD, holy convocations which you shall proclaim at their appointed times." Leviticus 23:2,4*

Each of the seven Feasts also marked specific milestones in the building work of Yahweh's House—the Foundation Stone laid in *the Passover Feast,* the Cornerstone set in at *Shavaot Pentecost,* and the Headstone that will complete it at the *Feast of Tabernacles: Sukkot (See my books, The Blueprint & Israel My Son).*

THE FEASTS OF GOD

God decreed the *new moon* of the month of Nisan as the beginning of months, initiating the beginning of the New Year. On the 14th day of this month, the Passover Feast was to be held—a revelation of the born-again experience, and new life gained from partaking of Jesus, our *Passover Lamb.*

> *"...the LORD gave the following instructions to Moses and Aaron: "From now on, this month will be the first month of the year for you." Exodus 12:1-2*

> *"On the fourteenth day of the first month at twilight is the LORD's Passover." Leviticus 23:5*

The Passover Feast represented redemption found only in Christ. It initiated the commencement of the building work of God's House in a corporate people, when Moses, as instructed by God, led them out of the bondage of Egypt into the transcendent work of Almighty God.

> *"And let them make me a sanctuary, that I may dwell in their midst. Exactly as I show you concerning the pattern of the tabernacle, and of all its furniture, so you shall make it." Exodus 25:8*

The nation's gathering and fellowship with God were reflected in the seven Feasts ordained by God where they were called to gather before Him. Paul and the apostles honored the Feasts in obedience to God's Word in the fear of the Lord.

> *"...but took leave of them, saying, "I must by all means keep this coming feast in Jerusalem; but I will return again to you, God willing." Acts 18:21*

> *"Therefore let us keep the feast, not with old leaven, nor with the leaven of malice and wickedness, but with the unleavened bread of sincerity and truth. Indeed Christ, our Passover, was sacrificed for us." 1 Corinthians 5:7-8*

Over History, God has remained faithful to His plan for the specific days He ordained for the fulfillment of each feast—from Passover through to Pentecost. As was promised to Israel through the prophet Joel, the Holy Spirit came and was poured out on the Jews gathered in Jerusalem for *Shavaot*—also known as Pentecost. Pentecost is the Greek word for fifty, representing the number of days God said to count, from Passover up to the beginning of *Pentecost*. History shifted dramatically when the Blessings of this Feast were later opened to Gentiles. The Holy Spirit fell on the gathering in Cornelius's House after Christ was shared with them, marking the entrance of a harvest of Gentiles chosen to be grafted into the Commonwealth of Israel (Acts 10:34, Eph. 2:12). God intended to make of the two—Jew and Gentile—*one new man.*

"...blindness in part has happened to Israel **UNTIL** the fullness of the Gentiles has come in. and so all Israel will be saved, as it is written: "THE DELIVERER WILL COME OUT OF ZION, AND HE WILL TURN AWAY UNGODLINESS FROM JACOB; FOR THIS IS MY COVENANT WITH THEM WHEN I TAKE AWAY THEIR SINS." Romans 11:25-27

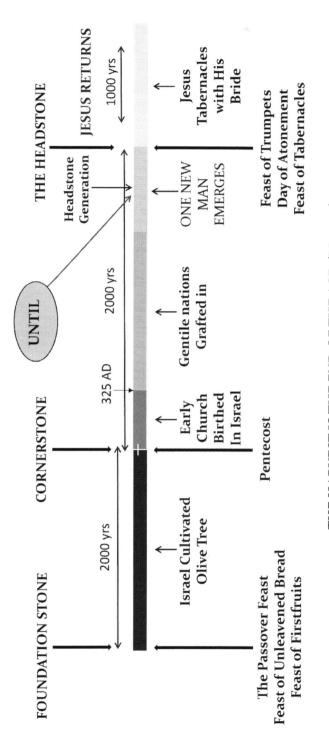

FOUNDATION STONE

CORNERSTONE

THE HEADSTONE

2000 yrs

Pentecost

UNTIL

325 AD

2000 yrs

Headstone Generation

JESUS RETURNS

1000 yrs

Israel Cultivated Olive Tree

Early Church Birthed In Israel

Gentile nations Grafted in

ONE NEW MAN EMERGES

Jesus Tabernacles with His Bride

The Passover Feast
Feast of Unleavened Bread
Feast of Firstfruits

Feast of Trumpets
Day of Atonement
Feast of Tabernacles

THE HARVEST IS THE END OF THE AGE (Matt. 13)

At the time of the fulfillment of the fall Feasts, the trumpets will resound at the *Feast of Trumpets on* the *new moon*, initiating the seventh month of *Tishri (Rosh Hashanah).* They will announce the *Return of the King* to the seat of His Throne in Jerusalem, and pronounce the completion of the LORD's work on His House!

The *Feasts of Yahweh* are heightened times in the Spirit, pregnant with revelations of the supernatural, spiritual dimensions of Christ. They are very much related to time and the Great Journey mapped out by God for His people. During the Feasts, Heaven draws close, and portals are opened on Earth for Angel Armies to marshal the momentum of His Plan gained on the ordained trajectory. The Feasts were designed by God to keep His people from straying off the path of His will as they followed obediently in the fear of the LORD. The Feasts are appointed times for coming before God's Presence, for passing before Him through these checkpoints where He assesses, evaluates, and releases the obedient to continue moving on to greater levels of Glory—*from Glory to Glory, to Everlasting Glory!*

After Pentecost, he early band of Jewish disciples moved out to accomplish great feats for the Lord, taking the Gospel of Jesus into the known world where multitudes were given entrance into the Kingdom of God. The roots of Christianity began to go deep as the foundation of God's Word was preached with demonstrations of power, signs, and wonders. However, the momentum of this holy movement was soon to falter. Satan was able to create a breach and hijack the new Church, just over three hundred years old. This occurred with the supposed conversion of Constantine Emporer of Rome.

CONSTANTINE AND THE ROMAN CHURCH

To close the breach that occurred in the early Church, we must first look to the root where the breach first occurred. To understand how the foundations that were laid in the House of

God got dismantled, and the Blueprint changed, we must look to Rome.

Mixture with the world entered the House of God when the first division occurred at the *Council of Nicea* in A.D. 325—convened by the emperor Constantine. This became the first official church council assembled to establish the doctrines of the new Roman church. Here they took the opportunity to split away from Israel—*the founding fathers of the Church*, in a dispute over the *Passover Feast.*

> *"From the Letter of the Emperor [Constantine] to all those not present at the council (Eusebius Vita Cons., Lib, III, 18-20)...*
>
> *It was declared to be particularly unworthy for this, the holiest of festivals, to follow the customs of the Jews, who had soiled their hands with the most fearful of crimes, and whose minds were blinded. In rejecting their customs, we may transmit to our descendants the legitimate mode of celebrating Easter; which we have observed from the time of the Savior's passion (according to the day of the week).*
>
> *We ought not therefore to have anything in common with the Jew, for the Savior has shown us another way; our worship following a more legitimate and more convenient course (the order of the days of the week): And consequently, in unanimously adopting this mode, we desire, brethren, to separate ourselves from the detestable company of the Jew.*
>
> *For it is truly shameful for us to hear them boast that without direction we could not keep the feast. How can they be in the right, they who, after the death of the Savior, have no longer been led by reason but by wild violence, as their delusion may urge them?...*
>
> *But even if this were not so, It would still be your duty not to tarnish your soul by communication with such wicked people [the Jews]. You should consider not only that the number of churches in these provinces makes a majority, but also that it is right to demand that our reason approves, and that we should have nothing in common with the Jews, (The Nicean and Post-*

Nicean Fathers, Vol. XIV, William B. Eerdsman Publishing Company, 1979, pgs. 54-55).

God has not given anyone the right or authority to change any of the ordinances of His written Word or the dates of His Feasts, as all were Divinely ordered to be fulfilled in their *set appointed time.* Constantine though credited with the Christianization of the Roman empire, nevertheless, was pivotal in transforming the face of Christianity with Rome's brand. He changed the dates of the ordinances and introduced a defiling mixture of the pagan idols he worshipped such as the *Sol Invictus,* the Sun God. In worship and honor of the sun, Constantine declared Sunday as the Roman Church's new Sabbath. The keeping of the Sabbath was established within the *Ten Commandments* of God given to Moses as an eternal ordinance.

Christianity under Constantine became a forced religion, and gatherings were allowed only in the Roman church buildings. Gatherings in homes were banned to contain heresies outside of the Roman church teachings. Only the priesthood were allowed access the the scriptures.

Constantine rejected the Jews and outlawed all biblical Feasts, the Sabbath, and anything to do with the Jews. He outlawed the Passover Feast and instituted Easter in its place—a day that honored the goddess *Ishtar.* He separated the Church from the Hebraic roots it was founded on while continuing to embrace paganism. If you think you have the authority to change one thing in God's Word, you will think you have the authority to change anything. Satan is the spirit behind the corruption of God's Word.

"And he shall speak words against the Most High [God] and shall wear out the saints of the Most High and think to change the time [of sacred feasts and holy days] and the law; and the saints shall be given into his hand for a time, two times, and half a time [three and one-half years]." Daniel 7:25 AMP
(The word times in this passage is zeman and means the appointed occasions)

The establishment and continued celebration of Easter sits as a rejection of Israel, and the honored place given by God to Israel. Easter is a repudiation of the contract made between God and Israel, that the nation would stand before Him as an everlasting praise on Earth in which His House is established.

"But Israel shall be saved by the LORD With an everlasting salvation; You shall not be ashamed or disgraced Forever and ever." Isaiah 45:17

"Son of man, this is the place of My throne and the place of the soles of My feet, where I will dwell in the midst of the children of Israel forever." Ezekiel 43:7

Rome chose to seize control of the Christian *movement* from the hands of the *Jews* and created a *religion*. They usurped the place of honor assigned to Israel and made the choice to replace Israel. Jerusalem—the City of God, the Lord's resting place forever, the Seat of His Throne, and the administrations of His Kingdom was replaced by Rome. Their intent was also to assume control of the City of Jerusalem as part of their religious empire. Jesus is returning to Jerusalem where His feet are planted forever; no other City but Jerusalem is eternal. In the book dedicated to the early Roman church before Constantine, God saw what was to come in their future and gave a dire warning not to fall into this trap of the enemy.

"...do not boast against the branches. But if you do boast, remember that you do not support the root, but the root supports you. You will say then, "Branches were broken off that I might be grafted in." Well said. Because of unbelief they were broken off, and you stand by faith. Do not be haughty, but fear. For if God did not spare the natural branches, He may not spare you either."

"For if you were cut out of the olive tree which is wild by nature, and were grafted contrary to nature into a cultivated olive tree,

69

how much more will these, who are natural branches, be grafted into their own olive tree?"

"For I do not desire, brethren, that you should be ignorant of this mystery, lest you should be wise in your own opinion, that blindness in part has happened to Israel **until** *the fullness of the Gentiles has come in. And so all Israel will be saved, as it is written: "THE DELIVERER WILL COME OUT OF ZION, AND HE WILL TURN AWAY UNGODLINESS FROM JACOB; FOR THIS IS MY COVENANT WITH THEM, WHEN I TAKE AWAY THEIR SINS." Concerning the gospel they are enemies for your sake, but concerning the election they are beloved for the sake of the fathers. For the gifts and the calling of God are irrevocable." Romans 11:18-25*

The gifts and the calling of God are *irrevocable*—they are permanent and cannot be changed! The House of God must therefore be built according to the Blueprint established on the Hebraic foundations of the apostles and prophets. We are now crossing over into the times of the restoration of all things where God is beginning to rebuild and restore His House to His first intentions. God's Word emphatically declares that He will never abandon Israel and that He is not a man that He would lie. Jeremiah 33 declares three times that God will *restore the fortunes of Israel* and rebuild them!

"Thus says the LORD: If you can break my covenant with the day and my covenant with the night, so that day and night will not come at their appointed time, then also my covenant with David my servant may be broken... If I have not established my covenant with day and night and the fixed order of heaven and earth then I will reject the offspring of Jacob and David my servant..." Jeremiah 33:20, 25

When God has revealed His Word, to continue to follow *the way of Rome* is to participate in their deception and rebellion against His Word. God has tolerated much in His mercy and love toward the Gentile people of the world, *for a time,* to gather in a great Harvest of souls. With the level of antisemitic hatred throughout the centuries, the Gospel had to be made palatable to the Gentile nations. Nevertheless in the end, as the times of the summing up of all things in Christ begins, *all deception* will be exposed and will fall in the great shakings of the climax of the ages. All the ordinances of God are completed within Christ. The Word promises that nothing outside of the Jewish Messiah remains.

> *"See that you do not refuse Him who speaks. For if they did not escape who refused Him who spoke on earth, much more shall we not escape if we turn away from Him who speaks from heaven, whose voice then shook the earth; but now He has promised, saying, "YET ONCE MORE I SHAKE NOT ONLY THE EARTH, BUT ALSO HEAVEN." Now this, "YET ONCE MORE," indicates the removal of those things that are being shaken, as of things that are made, that the things which cannot be shaken may remain." Hebrews 12:25-27*

The things that are made, that are traditions created by man cannot stand and will be removed. If the foundation of a house is built on deception and lies at a minimum it will be unstable at the worst, it will collapse. The stage is being set for Jesus' return! everything outside of Him and His will, will be trampled and fall with a resounding crash. All Babylonian systems and influences built on deception will collapse. The Roman Church as it stands today, founded upon an unbiblical papacy with all its embedded idolatry, mixture, and sin, cannot stand before the Presence of the King of kings.

> *"I will make justice the measuring line and righteousness the plummet; and hail will sweep away the refuge of lies, and waters will overwhelm the hiding place (the shelter). And your covenant with death shall be annulled, and your agreement with Sheol (the place of the dead) shall not stand; when the overwhelming scourge passes through, then you will be trodden down by it." Isaiah 28:17 AMP*

THE ISSUE OF COLOSSIANS TWO

Easter is the feast of Ishtar or *Ashera*. God in His mercy will utilize anything that will bring souls to salvation, even Pagan holidays such as Easter. However, as the time draws near to Jesus' return all deception will be exposed by the Light. *A little leaven has the potential to leaven the whole lump.* The following words of Paul in Colossians have been used in an attempt to eliminate all traces of God's ordinances given to Israel. In the misunderstanding of what he was saying, the baby was thrown out with the bath water. Paul was addressing a variety of issues in this passage:

"So let no one judge you in food or in drink, or regarding a festival or a new moon or sabbaths, which are a shadow of things to come, but the substance is of Christ." Colossians 2:16-17

Let no one cheat you of your reward, taking delight in false humility and worship of angels, intruding into those things which he has not seen, vainly puffed up by his fleshly mind, and not holding fast to the Head, from whom all the body, nourished and knit together by joints and ligaments, grows with the increase that is from God. 18-19

Therefore, if you died with Christ from the basic principles of the world, why, as though living in the world, do you subject yourselves to regulations—"Do not touch, do not taste, do not handle," which all concern things which perish with the using—according to the commandments and doctrines of men? 2:20-22

In verses 16-17, Paul admonishes the people to not allow anyone to judge them in adhering to the *ordinances of God.* He explained that they *were* a shadow of things that were **yet to come**—some were fulfilled in Christ, some yet to come as in the final Feast days and the seventh-day Sabbath Rest of Christ's millennial reign.

In verses 18-19, Paul exposed the idolatry that had seeped in, as in the worship of angels, rather than holding fast to Christ the Head of the body, who alone is its nourishment. In verses 20-22, Paul makes clear that in Christ we are dead to the rudiments *of the world,* then asks the Colossians why they were submitting themselves to the *commandments and doctrines **of men.*** Traditions and rituals had come in from the Priesthood of that day, something that Jesus himself addressed.

> *"Their worship is nothing more than a charade! For they continue to insist that their man-made traditions are equal to the instructions of God.' "You abandon God's commandments just to keep men's rituals, such as ceremonially washing utensils, cups, and other things." Then he added, "How skillful you've become in rejecting God's law in order to maintain your man-made set of rules." Mark 7:9 TPT*

Traditions and commandments of men and a Pagan dynamic have influenced the Church *for* 2000 years. God did not intend for Gentiles to become Jews, or for either Jews or Gentiles to keep religious *rituals* that were fulfilled in Christ. However, apart from the rituals, there is to be an honoring of their representation in Christ and their significance as markers in God's work. We are to honor God's Word, what He has ordained, and what He honors!

The Feasts of God are God's Call for His people to gather corporately before His Presence, in acknowledgment that He is God, the great I AM, and *that there is none other*. Whenever the Feasts are celebrated, the truth of what they represent is prophetically declared until the time of their fulfillment. This should give great impetus for the celebration of the *Fall Feasts* fulfilled in Christ's return!

Our God surpasses anything that can be perceived and is worthy of all honor, praise, and obedience to His commands. His Presence and Glory *cause all to bow low and fall prostrate before Him!* The fear of the Lord is moving into His House to bring the changes required to set it on its rightful foundations. We cannot be as the rebellious, reserved for judgment, to whom God said: *"...the fear of Me is not in you"* (Jer. 2:19).

The Lord is calling us back to His way, and out from the traditions of men. God *has* never moved outside of Israel, the whole council of God is embedded within Israel and Jerusalem. The Jewish scriptures were the Bible of the early church, and are embedded within the letters that now form the New Testament. Jesus honored all the words of the prophets and quoted them often, and He honored the Feasts of God. In the fullness of time, God will move to supernaturally make of the Jew and Gentile, *one new man*. Israel's eyes will be opened and Gentiles will recognize God's great love for Israel. Together they will return to the foundations of the *apostles* and the *prophets*. The day will come when men will grab hold of a Jew as the way to God.

> *"Yes, many peoples and strong nations Shall come to seek the LORD of hosts in Jerusalem, And to pray before the LORD.' "Thus says the LORD of hosts: 'In those days ten men from every language of the nations shall grasp the sleeve of a Jewish man, saying, "Let us go with you, for we have heard that God is with you." Zech. 8:22-23*

The Leadership called forth to serve God in the Last Days will be required to teach and make the necessary changes to bring the House back into God's order. Just as Moses was, leaders today are charged with leading God's people to eat of the Passover Lamb and to leave Egypt. They will lead them out of the deceptive ways of the world, and idolatry to its gods, and lead them back to obedience to the Word of God.

Transformation *and* restoration will not happen apart from the agreement and unity of the leaders to begin to shift and turn away from paganism and idolatry in the church and turn back to obedience to God's way. As Israel was made blind to the Gospel until the fullness of the Gentiles becomes grafted in, so also the

Gentiles have been blinded to the truth of Israel and their place in the heart of God!

There cannot be *a* mixture of the holy things of God with that which is unholy. God m*ay have* tolerated *it* for a time and may *have even* use*d* it for his ends, but ultimately in His appointed time, all mixture will be removed. God will restore His House *birthed from His Heart,* to His original blueprint of Christianity— the Cross where all bow to His will and His Word.

In the following chapters, we will continue to explore the building blocks of God's House as it was built and continues to rise over history. We begin by examining four significant features—the foundation, the foundation of the superstructure, the superstructure, and the completion in the Headstone of the this transcendent edifice.

Chapter Seven

THE FOUNDATION

"Son of man, describe the temple to the house of Israel, that they may be ashamed of their iniquities; and let them measure the pattern. And if they are ashamed of all that they have done, make known to them the design of the temple and its arrangement, its exits and its entrances, its entire design and all its ordinances, all its forms and all its laws." Ezekiel 43:10-11

The Blueprint of God's Temple unveils the story of His unfolding plan over history, each stage founded within the confines of Israel and narrated in the life of *Jeshua, Son of Israel*. The Blueprint is otherworldly, as its design finds its origin in another realm. Its source is the very heart of God and manifests in Christ through the sacrifice of His life on the Cross.

The Temple was given birth through the spoken Word of God conveyed through the prophets. Consequently, it finds its genesis in the prophetic, underscoring the significant role attributed to the prophets in scripture—hence God's ominous warning, *"Do not touch my anointed ones: do my prophets no harm"* (2 Chron. 16:22).

The House of God consists of the Foundation, the foundation of the Superstructure, the Superstructure, and the Headstone. Over the next few chapters, we will explore these four distinct components, underscoring the pivotal role that Israel plays in each phase of God's overarching plan.

That Israel serves as the foundation for all of God's work on Earth, is a critical concept for all builders of God's House to grasp.

77

Paul stated that blindness has happened to Israel for a set *time*, completed in the fullness of times when the fullness of the Gentiles has come into the vessel that is, *the Israel of God.* It is within this context that the profound declaration resounds: "*...and so all Israel shall be saved!*" (Rom. 11:25-26, please see our books *Israel My Beloved* and *The Blueprint* on this most significant subject of our times.)

Jesus, the Son of God—born a Son of Israel, is the embodiment of the comprehensive Pattern of God's House. Over the centuries, compromise with worldly ideologies and human agendas infiltrated the Divine design of Yahweh's House. Relentless religious spirits have persistently sought to erode the dynamic, life-infusing power of God in each restorative movement of the Holy Spirit. The adversary's ongoing strategy is evident in his efforts to morph the life of Christ into a lifeless religion and ritual. This he achieved by introducing corrupting and defiling influences into God's House. His most significant achievements thus far lie in distorting the Word of God and challenging God's love and faithfulness to His people Israel. This distortion extends to the gross misrepresentation of the profound significance of Israel in the realization of God's overarching plans and purposes. The distortion extends to the establishment of *all five* of the five-fold ministry, and the key component of their assigned work *to build.*

> "*And He Himself gave some to be apostles, some prophets, some evangelists, and some pastors and teachers, for the equipping of the saints for the work of ministry, for the edifying of the body of Christ...*" Ephesians 4:12

The word *edify* is *oikodome*, related to architectural structures and means *to build.* A component of this Greek word is *oikos* which means *to build a home and a family.* These five ministries were given for building up the family name of Jeshua, initiated in Israel, including the grafted-in Gentiles. All are brought to a perfect union, to a Man of the stature of Christ, to His Headship and rule over all. The dynamic of Israel has been overlooked in the building work of God's House as outlined in Ephesians four. The *Body of Christ* is the *Body of Jeshua Messiah*, a Body prepared for Him within the people of Israel. Gentiles who were *far off* were invited into this Body and famiily.

> *"But now in Christ Jesus you who once were far off have been brought near by the blood of Christ. For He Himself is our peace, who has made both one, and has broken down the middle wall of separation, having abolished in His flesh the enmity, that is, the law of commandments contained in ordinances, so as to create in Himself ONE NEW MAN FROM THE TWO, THUS MAKING PEACE, AND THAT HE MIGHT RECONCILE THEM BOTH TO GOD IN ONE BODY through the cross, thereby putting to death the enmity." Ephesians 2:13 (emphasis mine)*

God's architectural plan for His House bestows honor upon Israel's integral role in the grand design. The reinstatement of their honored position is an essential element in the completing work of building Yahweh's House and preparing the Bride for the King's return in Glory. This is not optional! Rather, God's will is certain, and His design will manifest, undeterred by the multitude of objections raised.

> *"Theirs is the adoption as sons; theirs the divine glory, the covenants, the receiving of the law, the temple worship and the promises. Theirs are the patriarchs, and from them is traced the human ancestry of Christ, who is God over all, forever praised! Amen." Romans 9:4-5 NIV*

The Church has not received anything of Spiritual value apart from Israel. Every blessing bestowed upon us by God has been mediated through Israel. Whether in the past, present, or future, everything of God is channeled through Christ via Israel. The origins of everything—the Word of God, Jesus, and the giving of the Holy Spirit—are all rooted in Israel.

The hands of Israel have set the foundation for the singular, all-encompassing Temple, and as prophesied in Scripture, their hands will bring it to completion (Zech.4: 9). Israel was the first seed planted in the Holy Ground of Christ—they are the root and the firstfruit of a tree that is Holy to the Lord (Rom. 11:16, Deut. 14:2).

> *"For you are a holy people to the LORD your God, and the LORD has chosen you to be a people for Himself, a special treasure above all the peoples who are on the face of the earth."* *Deuteronomy 14:2*

The *model structure of the future*—the end-time Sanctuary of God, is designed with Israel as an integral component. Christ is the Temple of God and as coming through the posterity of Israel, as a Son of Israel, *is representative of Israel*. The meaning of the name Israel is *the one who rules as God, Prince of God*. Consequently, it is of paramount importance for the Gentile church to re-establish vibrant and authentic connections to their Hebraic roots.

Jesus, as both *the Root* and *the Branch* of Israel is central to Israel's constitution and structural fiber. In Scripture, Jesus is inherently identified with Israel as *one* in substance, call, and destiny:

- *Substance* – Deut. 18:5, Mic. 5:2, Ps. 34:20, Jo. 19:34-36, Rev. 22:16,
- *Call* – Hos. 11:1, Matt. 2:15, Jo. 4:22 Lk. 1:69, Acts 4:12 Is. 49:1-7, Acts13:47,
- *Destiny* – Zech. 14:4, Rev. 14:1-3, Is. 66:10-13, Rev. 22:1-5

> *"I am the Root and the Offspring of David, the Bright and Morning Star." Revelation 22:16*

Jesus was one with the people of Israel in Spirit from their beginning as a people and throughout their history. He was later born *into* Israel and is of the posterity *of* Israel. His Word was released *to them* through the prophets of Israel and as prophesied

He will return *to Israel*—His family, to rule and reign from Jerusalem according to Scripture (Zech. 14:4).

> *"Of this salvation the prophets have inquired and searched carefully, who prophesied of the grace that would come to you, searching what, or what manner of time, the Spirit of Christ who was in them was indicating when He testified beforehand the sufferings of Christ and the glories that would follow." 1Peter 1:11*

The *Foundation Stone* of the House of God is Christ, anchored securely and eternally *in Israel*. Each stage of its construction is Christ-centric, intricately woven into the fabric of Israel. Serving as the root of God's Olive tree, Israel stands as the sacrificial seed chosen for God's purposes in *Christ*—the Sacrificial Lamb of God. This Olive Tree, representing Christ rooted in Israel, serves humanity as the Divine conduit through which God channels all His sustenance, blessings, and inheritance to the world.

> *"After all, if you were cut out of an olive tree that is wild by nature, and contrary to nature were grafted into a cultivated olive tree, how much more readily will these, the natural branches, be grafted into their own olive tree!" Romans 11:24*

> *"May the LORD bless you from Zion all the days of your life; may you see the prosperity of Jerusalem..." Psalm 128:5*

LAYING THE FOUNDATION

As many different specialists work in the building of natural structures, so it is in the House of God. Some are called to work on foundations, and some on roofs and coverings. Others are called to work on the plumbing and the electricity—the water and power source. Yet, all will have some level of understanding of the various aspects of building the house. These many builders and specialists must work together to build the house—but there is only one Architect and one Blueprint they work from.

As Paul said, regarding the House of God, builders must be careful how they build on the foundation that *has been laid*. The foundation must be according to the Blueprint of the Word—built upon God's truth and precepts (1 Cor. 3:11).

In the construction of the House of God, *which is Christ*, a Divine plumbing system and pipeline is featured. The River of God often emphasized in revivals, is the very River that commenced its flow from Jerusalem, Israel, on the day of Pentecost. Its fullness will be realized upon completion of the House, *also from Jerusalem.* This conduit, fixed in Jerusalem, facilitates the unrestricted flow of the *River of the Water of Life*—the Word of God, throughout the entirety of the House, and out to the world (Ezekiel 47:3, Revelation 21:1).

Every house is also fitted with an electrical grid. In the House of God, Heaven's electrical grid is its power source. It is established in Christ who stands positioned within the portal of Israel. Designated by God, Israel serves as the power plant for transmitting power through Christ to the global *substations*—the worldwide assemblies connected to His Life. Transmission of power occurs along the *Lifeline of the Blood of Jesus*, facilitated by the Holy Spirit.

Jerusalem is the location of God's Heart beating in Christ, where the electrical impulses of His Power pulsate, generating Life throughout His Body. As the place of His Heart, Jerusalem became the place of the Cross, where the Blood of Jesus began to flow, reaching out to the nations of the world, and bringing Life to the Body of Messiah with every heartbeat. In the realm of the Body of Christ, the heartbeat of God resonates most powerfully when Israel is honored and blessed.

Both the plumbing and the electrical power source are located in the foundations of a house. In God's House, this is Israel. Wherever foundational teachings emphasize the profound significance of Israel within the fabric and DNA of the Body of

Christ, in such churches and ministries, you'll witness God's Heart pulsating with Life, Power, and anointing, producing great fruit for the Kingdom.

Conversely, where there is dishonor directed toward Israel or teachings about Israel that are in error, you will encounter an absence of God's power, anointing, and Presence. The void of the Holy Spirit's power becomes evident, for God has ordained Israel as the conduit of His blessings in Christ, bringing Life into the Body.

"I will bless those who bless you, and I will curse him who curses you; and in you all the families of the earth shall be blessed." Genesis 12:3

"Also the LORD your God will put all these curses on your enemies and on those who hate you, who persecuted you." Deuteronomy 30:7

"Rejoice with Jerusalem, And be glad with her, all you who love her; rejoice for joy with her, all you who mourn for her; that you may feed and be satisfied With the consolation of her bosom, That you may drink deeply and be delighted With the abundance of her glory." Isaiah 66:10-11

A foundation of honoring Israel in Ministries and churches can be established through a variety of ways such as: engaging in prayer and intercession, providing financial support, delivering anointed teachings, establishing and nurturing connections with individual Messianic congregations and leaders, and engaging in ministry directed toward the nation and people of Israel. Additionally, supporting ministries that, in turn, support Israel can further establish ties with the nation. These relationships and connections with Israel open channels for mutual blessing, a process that can begin in small ways and gradually expand into broader areas of connection.

"For it pleased those in Macedonia and Achaia to make certain contributions for the poor among the saints who are in Jerusalem. It pleased them indeed and they are their debtors. For if the Gentiles have been partakers of their spiritual things, their duty is also to minister to them in material things."
Romans 15:26

The foundation of Yahweh's House, that is *The Christ,* was firmly and supernaturally secured in Israel for all eternity by God its Architect. *Israel is forever!*

"And He said to me, "Son of man, this is the place of My throne and the place of the soles of My feet, where I will dwell in the midst of the children of Israel forever." Ezekiel 43:7

Chapter Eight

THE SUPERSTRUCTURE

"Whom will he teach knowledge? And whom will he make to understand the message? Those just weaned from milk? Those just drawn from the breasts? For precept must be upon precept, precept upon precept, Line upon line, line upon line, Here a little, there a little." Isaiah 28:10

In the context of a building or structure, the superstructure comprises the portion erected above the foundation that extends in depth beneath the ground. When applied to concepts, the term superstructure denotes the envisioned result emerging from established foundational precepts, encapsulating the culmination of a matter. In the context of the House of God, it is necessary to explore both perspectives within a Spiritual dynamic.

First, concerning the House of God, we must recognize that *Jesus is the conclusion of the matter!* He is both the Foundation and the Headstone, the beginning, and the end, and everything in between. Jesus became the visible manifestation of Truth and all foundational *precepts* instituted in the House of God, confirmed, and validated by the Father.

In the preceding chapter, we observed that *every* foundational principle of God was initially laid within the nation and people of Israel, forming the bedrock of the Temple's foundation. With the construction of this edifice, those foundational precepts manifested in Jesus upon His appearance *in Israel.* The New Covenant in Christ emerged as the Superstructure established upon the foundational precepts written in the Old Testament. The New Testament is the New Covenant prophesied by Jeremiah, fulfilled in the coming of the Messiah.

THE FOUNDATION OF THE SUPERSTRUCTURE

Within the architectural framework of the House of God, the inaugural phase of the Superstructure, embedded in the New Covenant, was marked by the coming of Christ—anchored in the House as *its Cornerstone*. The cornerstone is a distinctive stone set in the foundation of the superstructure of a building; it holds immense significance in that all other stones are set relative to this *one stone*. Traditionally, the cornerstones of buildings were ceremoniously laid with elaborate rituals, often featuring engravings with the recorded date of its institution.

In the House of God, the Cornerstone was laid and distinctly positioned in the foundation of the superstructure, with the crucifixion and resurrection of Christ. It was eternally secured with the outpouring of the Holy Spirit at the Feast of Pentecost. This moment marked the beginning of a profound invitation to humanity throughout subsequent centuries, to enter into the House and family of God.

In Hebrew, the word *cornerstone* literally means the *head of the corner*. Christ as the *Head of the Corner* is the pivotal point, from which all stones find their place within the grand architectural design. From this *central point,* subsequent levels of the building were constructed within the unfolding story of Christ over History.

> *"Jesus said to them, "Have you never read in the Scriptures: "'The stone the builders rejected has become the cornerstone; the Lord has done this, and it is marvelous in our eyes'?"*
> *Matthew 21:42*

The early Jewish assembly birthed in Christ, in Jerusalem, was built on the foundational precepts of the Jewish Messiah and the work He accomplished on the Cross. The work of the Cross and the establishment of the early Jewish church by the apostles is the foundational first phase of the Superstructure.

The Scriptures teach that the Church was built on the foundation of the apostles and the prophets, these were *all sons of Israel* who were entrusted with the Word of God and the message of the Cross. In addressing the Gentiles, Paul explained that the subsequent levels of the Edifice of God's House included Gentiles from all nations:

> *"Now, therefore, you are no longer strangers and foreigners, but fellow citizens with the saints and members of the household of God, having been built on the foundation of the apostles and prophets, Jesus Christ Himself being the chief cornerstone, in whom the whole building, being fitted together, grows into a holy temple in the Lord, in whom you also are being built together for a dwelling place of God in the Spirit." Ephesians 2:19-22*

According to scripture *the twelve Jewish apostles*, are the twelve foundations of *the wall* of the City of God, and *the twelve tribes of Israel* are *its gates*. Entrance into the City is through the *gates of Israel* constructed in the foundation of the Superstructure.

> *"Also she had a great and high wall with twelve gates, and twelve angels at the gates, and names written on them, which are the names of the twelve tribes of the children of Israel... Now the wall of the city had twelve foundations, and on them were the names of the twelve apostles of the Lamb." Revelation 21:12-14*

On the day of Pentecost, the Breath of the Holy Spirit ushered in the Life of God to a prepared people—*Jewish people*. It initiated a spiritual earthquake that cracked the hard stone of religion and released a great awakening where thousands became believers. The Light of Heaven shone on the Word of God unveiling and unlocking hidden truths buried for centuries under a religious spirit.

GOVERNANCE IN THE SUPERSTRUCTURE

The release of new revelation caused the tearing and rending of the old wineskin, giving way to the formation of a new governmental order integrated into the foundation of the Superstructure. The new governmental order was founded on the five-fold Ministry of Christ—the High Priest and Apostle of the Faith. Whenever the Blueprint was faithfully adhered to, it worked to forge a path on the trajectory into the new dynamic of Christ that changed world history. *A Savior had come!* It was a blueprint fashioned for a mind renewed in Christ to overcome the challenges it would face and withstand the assaults and warfare that would rise to halt its movement and growth. The new Wineskin came embedded with Power to wage an effective war against the Satanic kingdom.

The new governmental structure was both flexible and organic, providing structure and definition to the gathering of God's people. Conceived by Divine design, its purpose was twofold: first to safeguard and empower the saints against the relentless onslaught of demonic forces intent on their destruction. In stark contrast to the rigid and elevated hierarchy that defined the Jewish Priesthood of that era, the new structure was *dynamic*, filled with the *dunamis* Life of the Holy Spirit, and characterized by fresh virtues of humility, meekness, and courage.

Second, the emerging superstructure facilitated a dynamic conducive to the priesthood of all believers, as they were swept into the potent current of Christ's Destiny. Here the gifts and callings of the assembly were unlocked and given expression. The design was intentionally crafted to give room for the full manifestation of all gifts, embracing the ministry of believers of every age, from the young to the very old (Acts 2:17-18).

The emerging Superstructure was distinguished by movement rather than religious rigidity. It provided for the River of God to flow through the assembly freely, opening doors of opportunity to all believers in various realms of ministry and leadership. The new leadership played a role in advancing the saints' maturity through their example, by leading as fathers and mothers on a forward trajectory. These leaders embraced their roles as devoted servants and bondslaves of the Lord and wholeheartedly committed their lives to His Divine purposes. Through their passionate love and unwavering dedication to the Lord, they became pillars, fortifying and sustaining the Body on its journey of being built up in love. (Ephes. 4).

The emerging leaders of Christ's discipleship program embodied the fundamental qualities and eternal features of their Master. This new breed of leadership had a mindset that was *embedded in eternity* and fixed on the Kingdom of God, as opposed to the Jewish priesthood of the day whose minds were fixed on maintaining their positions. Without caution, the dynamic moves of the Holy Spirit become rigid and crystallized leading to a resurgence of religion, legalism, and a loss of Glory.

To maintain God's Divine order and flow, recognition of the necessity for certain leadership roles outlined by Him in Scripture, is critical. These roles, including apostles, prophets, evangelists, pastors, and teachers are all crucial. They are established by God in *various alignments* to support God's vision for each assembly in their times.

Throughout the centuries, and persisting into the present day, a notable portion of the church has chosen to disregard some of these functions, deeming them irrelevant in the post-Scripture canon era. However, it is crucial to acknowledge that God has not given anyone the permission or authority to dismiss any of these foundational leadership functions. Each role plays an integral part in fulfilling His Divine will for the conclusion of the ages. According to the Word of God, these five ministries were bestowed as gifts to the Church, to fulfill His work.

"And He Himself gave some to be apostles, some prophets, some evangelists, and some pastors and teachers, for the equipping of the saints for the work of ministry, for the edifying of the body of Christ..." Ephesians 4:11

Until all are fully restored and functioning as was intended by God, the full restoration of the House as God cannot be attained as He intended it. Through the various functions of these ministries, the Lord envisioned a fully equipped and mature Body undergoing Spiritual transformation. Through this process, it becomes a majestic Bride prepared and made ready for the return of her Bridegroom. As this Scripture says, *He Himself* gave these gifts to His Church.

"...till we all come to the unity of the faith and of the knowledge of the Son of God, to a perfect man, to the measure of the stature of the fullness of Christ..." Ephesians 4:11-13

It is also important to look at where these leadership roles and positions of governance, have undergone a distortion in their intended purpose and function. Rather than leadership *filled with the Holy Spirit*, serving the Body of Christ in the power of God, there can be a leaning toward man's natural abilities. The movement away from the original paradigm underscores the critical importance of a sustaining focus on Holy Spirit direction, revelation, and empowerment in all facets of leadership within the Body of Christ.

"So the churches were strengthened in the faith, and increased in number daily. Now when they had gone through Phrygia and the region of Galatia, they were forbidden by the Holy Spirit to preach the word in Asia. After they had come to Mysia, they tried to go into Bithynia, but the Spirit did not permit them." Act 16:6-7

Critical elements to prioritize in the context of governance are submission to the Holy Spirit, humility, love, and a persevering and enduring spirit. These qualities form the bedrock of effective and Spiritually grounded leadership within the Body of Christ. Focusing on these virtues ensures a leadership style that aligns with the principles of Christ and advances unity, service, and the well-being of the community.

Regarding leadership models, it is important to steer clear of excessive rigidity, dogmatism, and judgment of other models—*maintaining flexibility in the Holy Spirit is crucial.* The same God who can craft a myriad of songs from just seven musical notes may fashion varied leadership structures and alignments for a specific work. However, for the Body to mature to the full stature of Christ as He intends, each ministry or function should be secured within the assembly of God's people—whether internally or through external relationships with others.

The God who intricately and uniquely designs every snowflake and shapes each fingerprint demonstrates His profound love for diversity. The comprehensive structure, composition, and essence of the leadership teams within the *Model House of the future* will be exclusively determined by the Holy Spirit, the Builder of the House of God, however, the apostle and apostolic functions will be crucial for the completion of God's House.

While terminologies may differ, the assortment of fruit produced may take various forms, styles might diverge, and sizes can vary, the fundamental ingredients, functions, and fragrance will consistently remain *true to Him.* It is crucial not to restrict the Holy Spirit within the confines of any rigid pattern based on what might be observed in other churches. Yet, it is equally vital to ensure that foundational elements are represented in some form, allowing for a dynamic and diverse expression of the Spirit's work to be secured within the Body of Christ.

THE SUPERSTRUCTURE RISES OVER HISTORY

When Peter visited the House of Cornelius, by the command of the Holy Spirit, the door to the Gentile people of the world swung wide open. The Gentile gathering at Cornelius's house received the gift of the Holy Spirit—*a Gentile Pentecost!* The Edifice of the House of God then began to rise as Gentile peoples of the nations were baptized by the Holy Spirit into the structure. The superstructure began to rise ascending toward the Throne of God.

> *"While Peter was still speaking these words, the Holy Spirit fell upon all those who heard the word. And those of the circumcision who believed were astonished, as many as came with Peter, because the gift of the Holy Spirit had been poured out on the Gentiles also. For they heard them speak with tongues and magnify God." Acts 10:44-46*

The Superstructure of the House can be likened to the womb of the Body through which the Harvest of the nations of the world is given birth and gathered into the House. An assembly structured according to the Lord's Blueprint ensures that the foundational principles are secured in place.

The increasing momentum generated by the unrestricted flow of the Holy Spirit, will break forth from this womb and spill over onto the community, the nation, and the nations of the world. This is the natural progression of God's Life at work to gather out of the nations a people for Himself.

Should all the ingredients and foundational principles be in place and functioning as intended by the Lord, the community of God's people will be full of Holy Spirit life, continuous movement, and growth. Growth, in this context, may not manifest solely in numerical increase, it can also be reflected in reproduction as it spreads to different regions. Growth encompasses not only the expansion within the assembly of saints but also the multiplication of impact and influence through the establishment and support of other communities of faith (Acts 1:8).

(See our Book: The Blueprint for more diagrams)

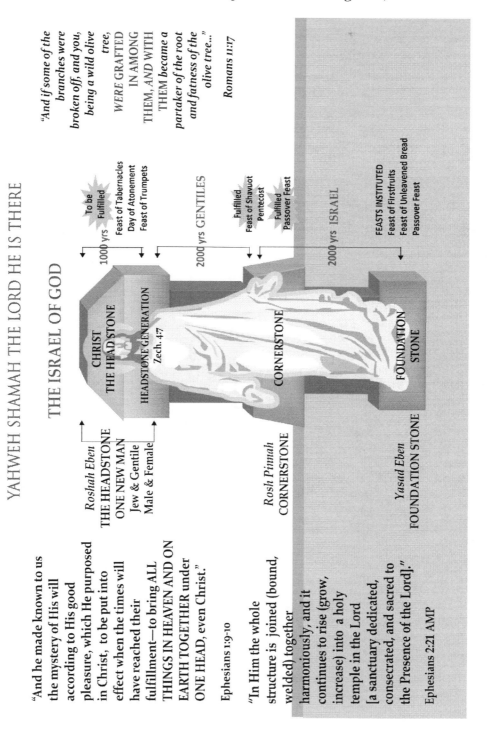

YAHWEH SHAMAH THE LORD HE IS THERE

THE ISRAEL OF GOD

"And if some of the branches were broken off, and you, being a wild olive tree, WERE GRAFTED IN AMONG THEM, AND WITH THEM became a partaker of the root and fatness of the olive tree..."

Romans 11:17

To be Fulfilled
Feast of Tabernacles
Day of Atonement
Feast of Trumpets

1000 yrs

Fulfilled
Feast of Shavuot
Pentecost

Fulfilled
Passover Feast

2000 yrs GENTILES

FEASTS INSTITUTED
Feast of Firstfruits
Feast of Unleavened Bread
Passover Feast

2000 yrs ISRAEL

CHRIST
THE HEADSTONE

HEADSTONE GENERATION
Zech. 4:7

CORNERSTONE

FOUNDATION
STONE

Roshah Eben
THE HEADSTONE
ONE NEW MAN
Jew & Gentile
Male & Female

Rosh Pinnah
CORNERSTONE

Yasad Eben
FOUNDATION STONE

"And he made known to us the mystery of His will according to His good pleasure, which He purposed in Christ, to be put into effect when the times will have reached their fulfillment—to bring ALL THINGS IN HEAVEN AND ON EARTH TOGETHER under ONE HEAD, even Christ."

Ephesians 1:9-10

"In Him the whole structure is joined (bound, welded) together harmoniously, and it continues to rise (grow, increase) into a holy temple in the Lord [a sanctuary dedicated, consecrated, and sacred to the Presence of the Lord]."

Ephesians 2:21 AMP

The Divine progression, launched from Israel and extended to the ends of the earth, was encapsulated in God's master plan. This plan gives full expression to the wisdom of God, as a large Harvest of Gentiles from all nations become grafted into Israel at the culmination of the age. Ultimately, as a profound expression of God's Divine design, all nations of the earth ascend to Jerusalem to worship the King.

"And it shall come to pass that everyone who is left of all the nations which came against Jerusalem shall go up from year to year to worship the King, the LORD of hosts, and to keep the Feast of Tabernacles." Zechariah 14:17

The essence of normal Christianity, as witnessed in the early church, reveals a dynamic *two-way flow*: as disciples go out to the nations with the Gospel, the nations, in turn, are gathered and grafted into the entity that is Israel. The power of the Gospel spreads and takes root in all cultures and peoples, supernaturally gathering them into the Kingdom of God's dear Son—Christ our Lord (Rom. 11:24-25, Col.1:13).

The assembling of God's people is presently undergoing a Divine reconstruction, returning it to the Pattern and Plumb Line of Christ prepared for transitioning into the Kingdom age and reign of the King. All mixture, distortion, and twisting of God's word will be dealt with by Him as He rises to take His place. The restoration of *His Blueprint* will encompass *all* His attributes and virtues, *especially His Jewish heritage*. As the Gentile church rises to choose, bless, and honor Israel, the Body then becomes aligned to Christ in His fullness, leading it to a state of health, strength, wholeness, completion, blessing, and power at the end of the Age.

Chapter Nine

THE HEADSTONE

"This is the word of the LORD unto Zerubbabel, saying, Not by might, nor by power, but by my spirit, saith the LORD of hosts. Who art thou, O great mountain? before Zerubbabel thou shalt become a plain: and he shall bring forth the headstone thereof with shoutings, crying, Grace, grace unto it." Zechariah 4:6-7 KJV

God has promised in His Word that He will complete that which He has started. The Headstone is the culmination of His work in the summing up of all things in Christ at the end of the age. It is the Final Stone laid by the very Hands of God that will complete the building work on the Temple prepared as a Bride for the return of Christ.

> *"Inasmuch as you saw that* **the stone** *was cut out of the mountain without hands, and that it broke in pieces the iron, the bronze, the clay, the silver, and the gold—the great God has made known to the king what will come to pass after this. The dream is certain, and its interpretation is sure." Daniel 2:45*

The Headstone should not be mistaken for the Cornerstone or the Foundation stone, as each represents the manifestation of Christ in the House of God in three distinct timeframes. The Headstone specifically denotes the *completion phase* of the Father's work on earth through His Son and within humanity. (Some Bible versions use the term "capstone" for headstone).

The completion phase of the work of God occurs in *the Day of the Lord,* when all things in Heaven and earth are gathered into

Him (Ephes. 1:10). The work of restoring all things to God's original intentions has begun, and is now moving the world toward the *Day of Completion*. It is therefore in the Church's best interests that its leaders understand the dynamics and features of these times. One thing is absolute: the Father's will shall be done. As the Firstfruit of many, Jesus will see the reward of His sacrifice—a company of passionate apostolic saints conformed to His Image. The apostolic/prophetic leaders and builders who prepare the Earth for Christ's second coming represent *the Headstone generation* equipped and made ready to serve His interests and intentions.

The whole counsel of God and all His intentions will be completed and summed up in Jesus His Son and executed through an apostolic/prophetic *headstone generation*, united to Him in purpose and will. This generation of leaders is now being formed in union with Jesus—who is *the Head Stone*. They have His Heart and Mind and are in full submission to the will of the Father. They are a body of passionate revolutionary end-time apostolic leaders and saints sent to prepare the way of the Lord. They are Christ's eunuchs who work with Him to prepare the Bride for their Master.

These men and women have been chosen for the hour, molded, and handcrafted by the Lord having certain characteristics. They will not flirt with the Bride or receive to themselves the Glory that rightfully belongs to the Bridegroom— they have gotten over themselves. They willingly sacrifice all for their King, including their lives, ensuring that He gets all the Glory.

Aaron, the High Priest, serves as a representation of Christ, His leaders, and all those engaged in ministering to the LORD and others. God commanded Aaron to wear a turban having a plate of pure gold, engraved with the words, "HOLINESS TO THE LORD." This symbolizes the sanctity and consecration of those called to serve Him (Ez.28:36-38). The Body of Christ is now comprised of a community of *priests and kings,* however, it's essential to recognize that God designates certain individuals as leaders to collaborate with Him in the construction of His Temple. He chooses specific individuals to represent Him as priests. They stand before Him, acting as conduits through whom His purposes are initiated and realized on Earth.

> *"For every high priest taken from among men is appointed for men in things pertaining to God, that he may offer both gifts and sacrifices for sin. He can have compassion on those who are ignorant and going astray, since he himself is subject to weakness.... And no man takes this honour to himself, but he who is called by God, just as Aaron was." Hebrews 5:1-4*

When leaders unite to bring forth the Headstone, symbolizing the *Most Holy Place* prepared for the LORD, the anointing oil released from their union flows down from Christ the Head, saturating the entire Body to align it with Christ. Subsequently, the Body willingly yields to the Mind of God, enabling Him to guide, form, and mold it into His Divine image. This unity gives rise to harmony and conformity to Christ throughout the Body.

> *"And he shall bring forth the headstone with shoutings of "Grace, grace to it!" Zechariah 4:7 NIV*

The word headstone in this translation is a combination of the two Hebrew words, *roshah*, and *eben*. *Eben* is the word *stone* and also means *to build*. The word *ben* means *son, as the builder of the family name, and* is also related to building the House of God. The stones in the building of God's House are all sons of God being built into God's Family through His Name.

Rosh, the masculine counterpart of the word *roshah*, is found in the Old Testament close to five hundred times and is usually translated as *head*. Notably, it is rendered in the feminine form in only one instance, in Zechariah 4:7 regarding *the headstone*. The Holy Spirit's choice to use the feminine form suggests a representation of the completion phase of the Body as it emerges in the form of His Bride. It gives also a revelation of the vast company of *women in Christ*, released in the closing days of this era. They will stand alongside men in the times of the summing up era of all things *in Christ* fulfilling many leadership roles *(See our book In His Image for more on God's purposes for women in this hour)*,

In alignment with the Hebrew definitions of the word *roshah, the* various English Bible translations, and also of other languages, carry multifaceted meanings all significant to God's work in the climax of the ages. These definitions contribute significant insight into the profound implications of this *headstone generation* in its portrayal of the concluding phase of God's work on earth and within humanity. Let's look at a few:

The Principal Stone

Principal: *First in rank or importance, predominant, prominent, primary, paramount, prevailing; principality of a nation ruled by a Prince.*

As the Principal Stone, the Headstone holds a position of preeminence, as it is governed by Jesus in its entirety and adorned with His Glory. Moreover, it stands predominant as a symbol of God's finished work in humanity through union with Christ Functioning as the Dwelling place of God, it is paramount in bearing the entirety of God's counsel.

The Cap Stone

A capstone is designed to cover and seal. The *Capstone* of God's House covers and seals the fullness of the finished work of the Temple. It is representative of the fullness of God—the fullness of Israel, the fullness of Christ, the fullness of Deity, and the fullness of the Gentiles coming in, grafted into Israel, *"...blindness in part has happened to Israel until the fullness of the Gentiles has come in" (Rom. 11:25).*

The word fullness is the Greek word *pleroma* from the root word *pleroo* meaning, *completion, a container filled up, crammed full to completion.* The Capsstone represents God's container sealed by God and with Christ.

The Chief Stone

As the Chief Stone, it holds ultimate authority to co-rule the nations with Christ, wielding a rod of iron as described in Revelation 2:26-27. This Stone embodies an apostolic army that is a mighty warrior and conqueror, functioning in union with the *Commander in Chief* who leads in unity with His army. It symbolizes *the Breaker* and carries the breaker anointing that rests on the head, going before the Body and leading it into a certain breakthrough and victory.

The Top Stone

The *Top Stone* is representative of the completion of the journey to the highest place—the pinnacle of Mt. Zion. It represents the Mountain of the Lord—the high and lofty place where we meet with God—high in His ideals, integrity, and righteousness. As the Word of God shows, the high places belong to God.

The Key Stone

Israel has been honored and granted a position at the forefront in the Head rather than in a subordinate role in the tail. The Keystone, housing the Key of David, is firmly set within Israel. This Key symbolizes access to God's Glory, serving as the means to open doors that none can shut and shut doors that none can open. The Keystone functions as the Key that will unlock the doors and entrance to a new era—*the Millennial reign of Christ.* The King has chosen to place His Keys within Israel, signifying the significant role the nation plays in His unfolding Divine plan.

The Last Stone

The Lord will complete what He started and present it as faultless (Jude 1:24). He is the Author and Finisher of the Faith. When the temples of God were completed in the Old Testament the treasures were brought in, the Presence then came, and the Glory descended and filled the Temple—Jesus was the *First Stone* and He is the *Last Stone* to complete His Temple, when the train of His robe fills the Temple.

Final Stone

The Final Stone laid by the Hands of the Father to complete the Temple of God *is Christ*. It is Christ in union with the final generation brought forth to prepare His way home to Israel. The Temple will be completed, and the Ark of His Presence will be ushered in:

> *"Then the priests brought in the ark of the covenant of the LORD to its place, into the inner sanctuary of the temple, to the Most Holy Place, under the wings of the cherubim."* 2 Chronicles 5:7

The Closing Stone

As the Closing Stone, the Headstone represents the closing of an era—*a two-thousand-year dispensation of Grace.* The Day of the Lord will come to close this door in a time of great tribulation and judgment on the Earth. Like Noah, God has been patiently at work building *The Christ*—the Ark of God for the salvation of the world. The day came when God told Noah and His family to get inside the ark; after seven days God *closed the door* and judgment of the earth began to cleanse it of iniquity.

> *"Then the Lord said to Noah, "Come into the ark, you and all your household...For after seven more days I will cause it to rain on the earth forty days and forty nights, and I will destroy from the face of the earth all living things that I have made... NKJV*
>
> *...male and female of each kind entered, just as God had commanded Noah. Then the LORD closed the door behind them." Genesis 7:4,16 NLT*

Chapter Ten

THE HEADSTONE DYNAMIC

"...and he shall bring forth the headstone thereof with shoutings, crying, Grace, grace unto it. Moreover the word of the LORD came unto me, saying, The hands of Zerubbabel have laid the foundation of this house; his hands shall also finish it; and thou shalt know that the LORD of hosts hath sent me unto you." Zechariah 4:7-9

The times of the summing up of all things in Christ bear the weight of a distinctive *end-of-times* dynamic that calls for the sons of God to take their place on the world scene. The emergence of this Headstone generation is central to God's Divine plan as they are called and prepared to serve Him within this paradigm. The Headstone dynamic depicts God's wisdom, strength, power, and resilience in a people, particularly in the face of the unprecedented challenges specific to this hour.

This Stone will showcase God's attributes in His end-time army, demonstrating strategic approaches, critical thinking, and innovative supernatural ideas that mark this phase of His work. Effective anointed leadership, endowed with such skills, will be essential to counter the intense deception and propaganda defining this critical hour. Meeting these challenges necessitates God's leadership to attain the stature of Christ, securely anchored in Him through a deep, unshakeable connection. Throughout this time, various features of the Lord will be highlighted, providing a framework for navigating and understanding the complexities of His unfolding Divine plan. Let's look at a few:

Kingdom Authority: The Headstone leadership will possess the fullness of authority to punish all disobedience by the completeness of *their obedience.* This chosen generation of leaders plays a pivotal role in executing the Divine assignment to work with the Lord in releasing the Spirit of Life in every sphere. Weighted with authority, they are tasked to complete the House of God with His Divine decrees *(2 Cor. 10:6).* Increased supernatural power will be granted to this *apostolic generation* to fulfill the mandate of preparing the way for the Lord and making straight the highway for His Return.

"The voice of one crying in the wilderness: "Prepare the way of the LORD; Make straight in the desert A highway for our God. Every valley shall be exalted And every mountain and hill brought low; The crooked places shall be made straight And the rough places smooth; The glory of the LORD shall be revealed, And all flesh shall see it together; For the mouth of the LORD has spoken." Isaiah 40:5

Strength to stand resolute: Inherent in the Headstone dynamic is the capacity to resist the temptation to compromise on God's interests and purposes, and to maintain steadfast commitment and unyielding strength.

"Behold, I have made your face strong against their faces, and your forehead strong against their foreheads. Like adamant stone, harder than flint, I have made your forehead; do not be afraid of them, nor be dismayed at their looks..." Ezekiel 3:9

Adamant: Unshakable in purpose, determination, or opinion; unyielding. A legendary stone said to be impenetrable, often identified with the diamond or loadstone (Word English Dictionary).

The Headstone is fashioned and formed with strength like *adamant stone*—a material known for its unbreakable and utmost hardness. The term *adamant* also conveys qualities of being unyielding and resistant to persuasion, signifying the strength of character in the power of the LORD. The place of governance firmly resides in the adamant Headstone in union with Christ.

The Mountain of the Lord: The Headstone represents the climb to the pinnacle of the Mountain of the Lord where He meets with His apostolic leaders. Its span and reach extend to the very Throne of God where power with God is received to execute His will! The Headstone denotes governance over mountains and spheres having sway over the Earth. It is positioned by God in the *overlap* of two eras, defined by *the powers of the age to come (Heb. 6:5).*

> *"...the mountain of the LORD's HOUSE shall be established on top [rosh - the HEAD] of the mountains, and shall be exalted above the hills, and all nations shall flow to it." Isaiah 2:2*

Faithfulness: In the time of its emergence, the Headstone portrays a Zadok-type priesthood, known for being unwavering in its faithfulness, especially during times of turmoil. Those associated with the Headstone are endowed with ears attuned to hearing, living in constant connection to the heart of God. This signifies a profound level of spiritual sensitivity and devotion having been gained, echoing the faithful attributes of this priesthood.

> *"However, the Levitical priests of the family of Zadok continued to minister faithfully in the Temple when Israel abandoned me for idols. These men will serve as my ministers. They will stand in my presence and offer the fat and blood of the sacrifices, says the Sovereign LORD." Ezekiel 44:15 NLT*

Anointed Ones: The work of God to bring His leadership to the place of authentic humility, brokenness, and submission to His will, releases the beautiful perfume of humility. This allows the release of the fullness of the anointing of Christ to rest on them. This anointing comes forth from the union of Jewish and Gentile servants in the embrace of God's will. This union produces *One*

New Man rising in the power of fresh oil poured out on them, to the Praise of the Messiah.

> *"Do not despise these small beginnings, for the LORD rejoices to see the work begin, to see the plumb line in Zerubbabel's hand." (The seven lamps represent the eyes of the LORD that search all around the world.) Then I asked the angel, "What are these two olive trees on each side of the lampstand, and what are the two olive branches that pour out golden oil through two gold tubes?" "Don't you know?" he asked. "No, my lord," I replied. Then he said to me, "They represent the two anointed ones who stand in the court of the Lord of all the earth." Zechariah 4:10-14 NLT*

Accurately Structured: The Headstone generation of apostolic leaders will have grown up to the Head, to the stature of Christ by their obedience to His precepts and the protocols of the Kingdom. Through submission to His work in their hearts, they become rightly aligned with the Plumb Line of His mind, heart, and movements.

> *"Behold, the Lord stood on a wall made with a plumb line, with a plumb line in His hand. And the LORD said to me, "Amos, what do you see?" And I said, "A plumb line." Then the Lord said: "Behold, I am setting a plumb line in the midst of my people Israel." Amos 7:7-9*

The Army of God: The army of God that will work with the Lord to conclude the Age, is the Headstone generation embedded with *the Shout of the King.* The Lion of Judah roars over His purposes on the Earth through this Vanguard. He wars against His enemies to break down barriers to His will. The Breaker anointing, similar to the coming of the fiery tongues that rested on the heads of the early apostles, signifies the empowering force with which He equips His chosen ones.

> *"The breaker is come up before them: they have broken up, and have passed through the gate, and are gone out by it: and their*

king shall pass before them, and the LORD ON THE HEAD OF THEM." Micah 2:13 KJV (emphasis mine)

The Harvest is From the Headstone: The Harvest is birthed from the maturity and union that is represented in the Headstone. The Harvest is made ready at the time of the maturity of the Headstone. It holds the Harvest at the end of the age and is the container that has become the Ark of God by its union with Christ. With the coming forth of a Headstone generation of leaders in the maturity of sons, conformed to the image of Christ, God brings forth a spectacular supernatural Harvest in and through the ministry of their lives.

"For the earth yields crops by itself: first the blade, then the head, after that the full grain in the head. But when the grain ripens, immediately he puts in the sickle, BECAUSE THE HARVEST HAS COME." Mark 4:26-29 (emphasis mine)

"The field is the world, the good seeds are the sons of the kingdom, but the tares are the sons of the wicked one. The enemy who sowed them is the devil; THE HARVEST IS THE END OF THE AGE..." Matthew 13:38-39 (emphasis mine)

The Fullness of Deity: The Headstone in Zechariah 4:7 is consistent with the stone laid before Joshua in chapter 3:9 where it is described as having seven eyes with the inscription, *"And I will remove the iniquity of that land in one day."* This inscription is a revelation of the scale of the abundance of Grace and power released by God upon the *Headstone generation* to finish His work to complete the Temple of the Lord and to rule and reign with Him—*it shall come forth with shouts of grace, grace to it!*

"Who art thou, O great mountain? Before Zerubbabel thou shalt become a plain; and he shall bring forth THE HEADSTONE thereof with shoutings, crying, Grace, grace unto it.!" Zechariah 4:7 KJV

"For behold, THE STONE that I have laid before Joshua: Upon the stone are SEVEN EYES." Zechariah 3:9

"For who has despised the day of small things? For THESE SEVEN rejoice to see the PLUMB LINE (separated stone) in the hand of Zerubbabel. They are the EYES OF THE LORD, Which scan to and fro throughout the whole earth." Zechariah 4:10

"And I looked, and behold, in the midst of the throne and of the four living creatures, and in the midst of the elders, stood a Lamb as though it had been slain, having SEVEN HORNS and SEVEN EYES, which ARE THE SEVEN SPIRITS OF GOD sent out into all the earth." Revelation 5:6

"And from the throne proceeded lightnings, thunderings, and voices. SEVEN LAMPS of fire were burning before the throne, which are the SEVEN SPIRITS OF GOD." Revelation 4:5

"The SPIRIT OF THE LORD shall rest upon Him, the Spirit of wisdom and understanding, the Spirit of counsel and might, the Spirit of knowledge and of the fear of the LORD. His delight is in the fear of the LORD..." Isaiah 11:2-3 (emphasis mine in all scripture)

The Lamb in union with the Headstone possesses seven eyes symbolizing the seven-fold spirit of God. The Lamb has seven horns on its head demonstrating complete power and authority over the Earth. Likewise, the Lamb is described as having seven Spirits, representing the comprehensive counsels of God displayed through the seven Spirits of Yahweh.

The Headstone has been granted eyes to see because it has learned to bow. It is comprised of an army of apostolic leaders who have come forth from the Crucible of Fire in great humility and submission to the will of God. In union with Christ, they represent the *Plumb line* at work to complete the end-time work of God. God brought forth such a company to begin His work and He will again have such a company to complete His work.

The Plumb line and the Headstone are in the hands of Israel and the Gentile Ekklesia working together as *One New Man*, or *The Israel of God*. They rejoice together when Israel is restored once again as a master builder to work with Messiah on the completion phase of the Temple.

The restoration of Israel, occurring in union with a body of Gentile saints during the *times of restoration*, will become the catalyst for the renewed release of the Commanded Blessing—the *'Promise of the Father.'* The Power of God will course through His assembly of saints, releasing immense grace to construct and bring forth this generation of apostolic leaders. As friends of the Bridegroom, these builders will diligently labor together to propel the Body into maturity, create a dwelling place for the incoming harvest of souls, and bring the Temple of God to completion as His Bride, "...*upon* **one stone** *shall be seven eyes*" (Zech. 3:9).

The Hebrew word *echad*, meaning *one*, also means *united*, and is from a root word meaning *unify*. The unity in this *one stone* will be a wondrous sign to the world and symbolic of things to come— it will be a miracle wrought by God, and a precursor of things that are about to take place.

The inscription on the *'separated one stone'* declares a profound promise—that God will remove the iniquity of the land in a single day. This land signifies the collective corporate Body of Christ in union with Israel. The anticipation is that as leaders come into this union and the Glory cloud fills this temple, the iniquity of this united land will be removed in accordance with God's Divine promise. This envisions a powerfully transformative and purifying work in the Body of Christ.

The unified Headstone depicts the formation of a singular stone carved in the image of Christ. In its union, this stone possesses the power to bring the final destruction to the image of the beast. This imagery suggests a powerful force imbued with

Divine purpose to overcome and replace any semblance of the opposing forces symbolized by the image of the beast.

"Inasmuch as you saw that the stone was cut out of the mountain without hands, and that it broke in pieces the iron, the bronze, the clay, the silver, and the gold—the great God has made known to the king what will come to pass after this. The dream is certain, and its interpretation is sure." Daniel 2:45

The Headstone the Sanctuary of His Eternal Rest: On the seventh Day of Rest, God will have finished His transcendent and surpassing plan to create for Himself a Temple, a House, a Family, a Bride—the Place of His eternal Rest!

"Arise, O Lord, to Your resting place, You and the ark of Your strength. Let Your priests be clothed with righteousness, and let Your saints shout for joy." Psalm 132:8-9

"The Spirit lifted me up and brought me into the inner court; and behold, the glory of the LORD filled the temple. Then I heard Him speaking to me from the temple, while a man stood beside me. And He said to me,

"Son of man, this is the place of My throne and the place of the soles of My feet, where I will dwell in the midst of the children of Israel forever." Ezekiel 43:5-7

Chapter Eleven

CHURCH OF THE FUTURE

"You became imitators of us and of the LORD; in spite of severe suffering, you welcomed the message with joy given by the Holy Spirit. And so you became a model to all believers in Macedonia and Achaia (NIV). For from you the word of the LORD has sounded forth, not only in Macedonia and Achaia, but also in every place."
1Thessalonian 1:6 NKJV

Jesus is *the House of God* and He alone, by His Holy Spirit, builds His House. Everything is from Him, through Him, and to Him. When Ezekiel's Temple was completed according to God's Blueprint, the Glory of God filled the Temple. The River of God was then released from the Throne to flow to the nations of the world. Many may have their ideas, opinions, plans, and agendas, but if they do not have *eternity* stamped on them, they accomplish nothing of eternal value. It is important to be utterly in subjection to the Holy Spirit as He is now dispatching His builders with the Blueprint and directions to build 'The Christ.'

There was a period in my life, while writing this book twenty-two years ago that I was forced by circumstances to take a job in a store that was part of a chain of major department stores. I was not happy about the job, but it seemed that this was where God wanted me to be. I was soon to find out why. The marketing strategy for the particular store where I worked was given the name '*Store of the Future.*' I came to understand that this store was the *model store* for the chain. It had both a local management team and a '*Store of the Future*' team. These two teams worked together closely to test out new procedures, innovative ideas, cutting-edge technology, and unique methods of servicing the customer. After a period of testing these ideas, if approved they were then exported to the other locations. This pioneering store was pressing through to break new ground and move with the rapidly changing times. They intended to stay in the game and remain an economically sound and profitable *store for the future.'*

On an occasion, while sitting in the Lord's Presence, I heard the words, *"Church of the Future."* I quickly came to attention as I realized God was about to release an important revelation. He began to showcase models of various churches, when I heard, *"Model Church of the Future."* I was puzzled as to what He meant by a model church of the future. However, as I sat in His Presence for some time, I began to get some understanding. The word model is defined as:

> *A prototype, a preliminary version, a vessel to be reproduced, a place where the procedure is first tested before being implemented in others of like kind.*

A Model Church God showed me, was one that He has tried and proved *concerning a specific revelation of the Godhead.* It is one where strategies and modes of operation having their source in the Heart of Christ, are tested, tried, perfected, and sealed with God's approval, to then be released and reproduced for an appointed period of history.

God illustrated this principle to me through the life cycle of a seed. When a seed is planted in the ground, it decomposes in the darkness of the earth and essentially appears to die. However, with regular watering, new life emerges from the darkness, reaching toward the nourishing rays of the sun. If cared for, this seed will grow into the form *dictated by its DNA* implanted by the Creator. The seed possesses the ability to bear fruit and re-produce a replica possessing the essential nature and qualities of the original seed. This process is a principle evident throughout His Creation and established by God in His Word.

"Then God said, "Let the earth bring forth grass, the herb that yields seed, and the fruit tree that yields fruit according to its kind, whose seed is in itself, on the earth"; and it was so." Genesis 1:11

"Most assuredly, I say to you, unless a grain of wheat falls into the ground and dies, it remains alone; but if it dies, it produces much grain." John 12:24

This principle is also a strategy of Heaven's warfare God employs whenever He has chosen to introduce a fresh revelation or facet of Christ or to restore and re-establish a particular truth through a new move of the Holy Spirit, *(this could appear to be a fresh revelation or one the Body has not had the eyes to see before because of a lack of the foundational precepts that the revelation is established on).*

In past moves of the Spirit, it is apparent that God invaded a particular location that was prepared through fervent prayer and the *death experience* of the Cross. The old wineskin ruptured creating the Spiritual environment to receive an infusion of new wine, thus giving birth to a new and revolutionary paradigm.

God imparted to the model, a novel spiritual constitution designed to support a key facet of Christ into the ongoing construction of His House. As the Divine work takes root and goes through a process of testing and refinement, it becomes established in His House over time. The new work then reproduces *its kind*, serving as a model for replication and new plants. The outstanding features of the new model are exported to other churches, regions, and nations becoming embedded in the House of God.

God's work continues in His House to bring it to completion. Present and past wineskins are tearing to make way for the continuous flow of New Wine revelation—*the best reserved for the last Day.* This strategic progression is advancing toward the culmination of times, for the unveiling of the *Model Church of the*

Future, prepared for the ages to come. It is patterned after the *fullness* of the stature of Christ in Glory. Many churches around the world are now being prepared to become wineskins fashioned into God's end-time *model of the future.*

Understanding this process sheds light on the intense warfare, refining fire, and suffering that has worked to prepare many churches for the *death experience.* This work is necessary to birth an organism that has the potential to be molded and shaped into a Holy Sanctuary for the future reign of the King of Glory. Such places become the platforms upon which Christ will stand to rule and reign in the days of awakening, harvest, and preparation for Christ.

PAST MODEL CHURCHES GOD HAS BIRTHED

God has given birth to many model churches in the past. These churches have exported into the Body of Christ important revelations and facets of Christ. History has witnessed the birth of various models, many of which went on to become established as denominations.

We have seen the birth of Word-based churches, having a strong emphasis on the Word of God. There have been Charismatic-type models emphasizing the leading of the Holy Spirit and the nine gifts of the Spirit recorded in 1 Corinthians 12:4-11. In the second half of the last century, we saw the emergence of prophetic models whose emphasis was on teaching and impartation of the prophetic gift and raising and releasing prophets in the Body.

With an escalation of end-time warfare, a prophetic model emerged having a very militant edge with its focus on intercessory prayer and Spiritual warfare. This *beachhead* model was birthed by God to equip the Body of Christ for the great battles to be fought in present and future wars!

More recently we began to see the early stages of an end-time apostolic-type model forming whose emphasis is on emerging apostles and apostolic leadership. The apostolic model is timed by God for His work to *complete the House of God* and prepare the way for Christ! According to Scripture, the *foundation* of God's House is established on the *apostles and prophets.* Completion will also be accomplished through the work of the *apostolic/prophetic model* brought forth in the Last Days. This model is built on the foundation of past models as the building work presses onward and upward in the Presence and fullness of Christ the Head.

These past models have all reflected Christ *"in part."* The Lord gave birth to each model to re-*store* within His Body large deposits of a specific facet and element of Christ's being, with the intention that its essence would permeate the *entire whole.* None of these models, in themselves, are the ideal. These models were birthed for a specific purpose, for a specific season of time, to mature and build the House of God.

As models became crystallized into rigid structures over time, the Glory present at their birth began to wane. In the height of their glory, each of these models served as the basis from which God worked to shape His House. God is always on the move, and leaders and builders are called to be flexible and to move with Him into greater depths of the revelation of the dimensions of Christ.

In recent years, in a Divine and beautiful way, many of these models of the past have begun taking on features of each other, as they have surrendered to God's work and the movements of the Holy Spirit. Eyes are being opened *to see* as the Body undergoes its metamorphosis into becoming conformed to Christ and *one* with the Father. These models that have emerged over His-story have served as a road map directing the people of God toward *the Model Church for the future,* constraining us on our ascent toward *'the perfect'*—the completed model of *'The Christ.'*

The two most recent models to have emerged—the beachhead model and the apostolic model, are two we will examine, as they are very important to God's purposes in this present hour and for summing up all things in Him. These models have embraced the best of past models and possess some features for the *Model Church of the Future.*

THE BEACHHEAD MODEL

A beachhead is a fortified position established by invading forces. Heaven has been invading Earth and establishing fortified positions as bases of operations in a campaign strategy to conquer and occupy the kingdoms of this world. The word *base* is defined as *a part that supports from beneath, a place from which an operation is directed.* We will look at these definitions in both the beachhead model and the apostolic model.

A beachhead church serves and supports the Body through intercession and prayer. It also serves God as an army to establish His purposes through Spiritual warfare in *a concentration of force.* A beachhead church is characterized by war. While other churches may deny the aspect of spiritual warfare, this church is dug into the trenches waging war against the forces of darkness. They forge the path ahead for the saints' journey to possess the Promised Land of Christ, preparing a Highway for the Glory to come.

> *"Prepare the way of the LORD; make straight in the desert a highway for our God. Every valley shall be exalted and every mountain and hill brought low; the crooked places shall be made straight and the rough places smooth; the glory of the LORD shall be revealed..." Isaiah 40:2-5*

> *"Go through, go through the gates! Prepare the way for the people; build up, build up the highway!" Isaiah 62:10*

A beachhead church is a church that has been established by Heaven for specific wartime campaigns. Trials, tribulations, and storms surround this church as they have been trained and prepared *in* battles *for* great battles ahead. The specific feature of

Christ they impart is *the Lion of the tribe of Judah*—Christ our Warrior King, and Lord Sabaoth, the Lord of Heaven's Armies.

Some of Paul's greatest revelations of the Church and its warfare in the heavenly realms came through His letter to the church at Ephesus—a church that was established as a fortified base amid great demonic darkness (1 Cor. 15:32).

> *"Finally, my brethren, be strong in the Lord and in the power of His might. Put on the whole armor of God, that you may be able to stand against the wiles of the devil. For we do not wrestle against flesh and blood, but against principalities, against powers, against the rulers of the darkness of this age, against spiritual hosts of wickedness in the heavenly places. Therefore take up the whole armor of God, that you may be able to withstand in the evil day, and having done all, to stand."* Ephesians 6:10-13

The beachhead model is a *house of prayer* for all nations and is characterized by the prophet, intercessory prayer, and spiritual warfare. The prophetic and the establishment of the prophet is an important feature of this model as they are called to declare the Word of the Lord over that which He has purposed. They have a strong foundation and understanding of the Word of God with which to war. They embrace the walk of righteousness, cleansing, and having holy hands. Deliverance and holiness are emphasized in the approach of the Throne of Glory. Lessons have been learned through much testing, producing great brokenness and humility in these saints. They have grasped the principle that in the battle against *the prince of the power of the air*, there can be nothing of his nature in them.

Worship and praise are heavily emphasized in this model as praise is one of the most important weapons in warfare against the powers of darkness. God imparts to this model innovative war strategies and unique manifestations of anointing in warfare to equip His army, take ground, and enforce His will. Signs, wonders, miracles, and the Power of God are evident and at work through this model as the angelic armies are released to war alongside these churches.

Radical, passionate sold-out leaders and intercessors, willing to be living sacrifices, are drawn to these churches. The River of God flowing through this model releases God's Power bringing healing to the nations. To be trained as a soldier, to see, understand, and enter this level of warfare there must be a high level of brokenness, humility, and submission to the Holy Spirit.

Mainstream churches have a difficult time understanding much of what God is doing in and through this model. Prophets and prophetic acts have always seemed strange to many of God's people. Unless open to the supernatural work of the Holy Spirit, churches not of this model will reject God's work in these churches, as this level of warfare has not been their experience. Many claim that they do not see this type of warfare in the New Testament church. *But many do not see simply because they are not a threat to the enemy and their eyes have not been opened to see.*

The Scriptures state that the *entirety* or *sum* of God's word is Truth (Ps. 119:160). The Old Testament was the Bible of the saints of the New Testament. Much of the New Testament Scriptures has its source in the Old as it is the foundation. Therefore, regarding certain issues in the New Testament, there is a void, as the New assumes or takes for granted many of the precepts established in the Old. For example, some denominations don't allow musical instruments or certain forms of worship because they don't see it in the New Testament. Some don't tithe for the same reason. *Yet these eternal principles have already been firmly established in the Old Testament and do not have to be re-established.*

This is also true of spiritual warfare. The entire Old Testament from beginning to end establishes warfare as a foundational part of the lives of the children of God. Spiritual realities and strategies of war are evident, depicted in the natural warfare of God's people Israel. It is important to pray for the eyes of our hearts and our understanding to be opened to embrace all the *facets* of Christ—to see Him as both the Lamb *and the Lion*. He has come as the Lamb that was slain and we will see Him return as a Lion who will destroy all His enemies. Just as we are called to participate with Him in His ministry as the Lamb, we are called to participate with Him in His ministry as the Lion.

This model of church is very important to Heaven's Last Day campaign to prepare the kingdoms of this world for the LORD and His Christ. They are the forty thousand warriors who crossover into the Promised Land as a vanguard. The saints who are drawn to and trained in such churches are especially dear to the Lord as they suffer much in their obedience to remain submitted to His will.

THE APOSTOLIC MODEL

The Scriptures declare that the Church is built on the foundation of the prophets and the apostles. Both the prophetic beachhead model and the apostolic model are bases of operations from which the Lord is presently working to build His Church. An evolution of apostolic models has emerged in past years working to prepare the Body of Christ for an *end-time model* to be brought forth for Christ's Return. Although these present models may differ from each other in certain ways, a feature common to all is the training, equipping, and releasing of leaders. Leadership and government are the emphases.

The apostolic model is characterized by sound, enduring leadership principles. This model is God's worksite where He chisels, molds, beats, and hammers out His chosen vessels to be sent out as builders and leaders in His work.

Leaders of the five-fold ministry are supernaturally drawn to this model where they are raised up, trained, and sent out. Establishing churches and Christ's commission to go to the nations is a foundational feature at the heart of this model. They serve as a base or Hub where apostolic five-fold teams make their home in their drive to serve the Body of Christ. They are willing to give of their sons and daughters to plant out to increase the Kingdom of God.

Submission is both taught and modeled, demonstrated through a *Divine apostolic order* that works to produce exponential growth. As the apostolic vision of the Kingdom is embraced corporately it creates an unconquerable atmosphere of unity in the community. These leaders are gifted as builders and overseers of the House of God having a corporate, global perspective of God's House. They carry an important anointing to establish union, are radically sold out to God, and are committed to serving His purposes.

On the negative side, in the past, there have been some movements that were heavy-handed and controlling, with leaders who insisted on submission to unbiblical tenets. Control is not God's way and we do not see this reflected in the ministry of the apostolic leaders of the early church, who *served* the Church, laboring to bring forth Christ in the saints.

Some past apostolic models have also rejected the manifestations and strangeness of the supernatural evident in the beachhead prophetic model. Apostolic teams who move only in wisdom void in the manifestation of God's power are in danger of shutting down the supernatural work and manifestation of the power and Presence of the Holy Spirit—*signs will always follow an authentic apostolic work.*

> *"Truly the signs of an apostle were accomplished among you with all perseverance, in signs and wonders and mighty deeds."*
> 2Corinthians 12:12

God is not divided. He gave birth to all models. The Apostolic and Prophetic models are beginning to unite under the Government of God's will, and the Government of His vision and purposes for this hour. There is an end-time *Model of the future* now emerging in the purity and holiness of God. It will be endued with Power from on High producing signs, wonders, and great miracles on the earth. This becomes a reality as the prophetic and apostolic *become one* in Christ. A body can run in strength and power wearing two different styles of shoes, but it will not run at all if one leg is missing. If the desire is to see the Glory of the Lord and be used to prepare His Way, the apostles and the prophets must begin running in sync to build the Temple of the Lord.

THE MODEL CHURCH OF THE FUTURE—THE HEADSTONE

The model Church of the future now coming forth is fashioned by God with a Kingdom mindset and will represent the *'whole'* counsel of God—Christ in all His fullness and Glory. It is a Model that is not afraid to adopt revolutionary methods initiated by the Holy Spirit, to guide and accelerate the saint's journey from salvation to union more efficiently in the last days. The Model of the future will be equipped and fully armed to guide the saints through the journey of trials and tribulation into the Promised Land of the Kingdom of God's Son.

The movement of God continually works to propel and accelerate His saints from Glory to Glory. Nothing is static in the Kingdom. The Church must, therefore, break free of mindsets ingrained in the past. These mindsets may have served God's purpose during a specific time but are no longer viable courses of action. This shift is necessary due to the nature of the current hour and the Body's progression into greater Light, revelation, and greater Glory—*the Power and fullness of the manifest Presence of God.*

The *Model Church of the future* will fully understand the complete journey having come through the fire of intense trials and cleansing. This Church of the Last Day will be defined by the Glory of God as His Presence will dwell there in fullness. From these houses of Glory, Christ will reign. These houses will fearlessly teach the full counsel of God, know the completeness of Christ, and have the fullness of the Holy Spirit without measure.

119

Model churches for the future will possess the best of both the *beachhead model* and the *apostolic model* as they become one with Christ. All the important and vital characteristics and features of past models are merging to produce this end-time model representing the *fullness* of *'The Christ.'* The full weight of God's Glory will rest on this Church.

This model will be well established in the Word of God with gifted apostolic teachers. It will serve the community and the nations reaching out with Power in evangelism to reap the Harvest. From it, the River of healing, deliverance, and counsel will flow. It will be gifted and anointed in intercessory prayer and powerful in authority and Spiritual warfare. It will be a church flowing in the prophetic in union with the apostles and serving as a base or Hub for teams of gifted apostolic leaders working together. It will be a Holy Place where the River of God flows in Power and strength. As all mixture has been removed, the angelic host will ascend and descend upon it and it resides under an open Heaven.

Through this *Model,* the Holy Spirit will give birth to innovative strategies *for the future* targeting the needs of the Harvest and the world. Strategic alliances will be formed with other hubs to facilitate the needs of the harvest and share the burden. Alliances will also be formed to engage the enemy to destroy strongholds and the works of darkness. This will be a model built on strong relationships within its community and with others in the Body.

> *"So Judah said to Simeon his brother, "Come up with me to my allotted territory, that we may fight against the Canaanites; and I will likewise go with you to your allotted territory." Judges 1:3*

It is imperative for the Church to now enter a Holy union to build this model for this hour. Emerging apostolic/prophetic leaders are gifts to the Body of Christ, that will lead it into the Promised Land of the Kingdom reign of Christ. This cannot happen until opinions, judgments, and agendas are laid on the Altar before God.

The Lord showed me a picture of the spaceship is a marvel of intricate and sophisticated design. It is created by numerous specialized teams dedicated to perfecting each component. Despite the complexity of the parts, each team must possess a comprehensive understanding and vision of the entire design. The integration of each part into the whole is crucial, as any missing or malfunctioning component will either prevent *liftoff* or result in a *mid-air explosion.*

Likewise, if there is not a *fellowship* of believers that function together and assemble as *one ship*, the ship remains grounded in earthly realms, unable to fully embody the Glories of its heavenly, eternal purpose. Self-centered agendas and the stress of the hour that is to come will cause its implosion.

God is now at work in the preparations to direct many streams into the *ocean of His fullness and His Glory*. These streams have served the King's purposes in a specific way for a certain time. God intends that the leaders allow Him to re-model the *ship* into a structure that possesses the supernatural dynamic to House the King of kings and support the full weight of His Glory. Not everyone will bow their knee to God's purposes and open the door to His knocking, but to those who do, *"...the King of glory shall come in"* (Ps. 24).

The necessity is for this model to now emerge, having a new dynamic suitable to the hour, a *model fashioned by God with the strength and nature to take us through to the future and the Ages to come.*

Chapter Twelve

ISRAEL & THE KINGDOM

"Of the increase of His government and peace There will be no end, Upon the throne of David and over His kingdom, To order it and establish it with judgment and justice From that time forward, even forever. The zeal of the Lord of hosts will perform this." Isaiah 9:7

To date, six structures have so far been erected to serve as dwellings for the Presence of God—*all erected within Israel.* These include Moses' Tabernacle, David's Tabernacle, the Temples of Solomon and Zerubbabel, and Herod's restoration of the temple over forty-six years. The sixth one—the Spiritual Temple of Grace, arose with the Resurrection of Jesus Christ to replace all previous ones. Each of these structures represented a distinct stage or chapter in the unfolding narrative of God's House constructed throughout history, illustrated through the Law, Worship, Glory, Mercy, and Grace. Herod's Temple, representing the futility of carnality in attempting to touch the things of God was the one destroyed by the Romans.

The seventh phase or structure of the Temple in the mystery of the ongoing *story* of Christ will be pure and Holy unto the Lord. It will be built without mixture from the defilement of flesh or the carnality of division and prejudice by saints who have chosen the way of the Cross. This Temple will be completed and united within the King in Glory by those who have ascended the hill of the Lord, having clean hands and pure hearts (see our book, *The Blueprint* for diagrams).

"Who may ascend into the hill of the LORD? Or who may stand in His holy place? He who has clean hands and a pure heart, Who has not lifted up his soul to an idol, Nor sworn deceitfully."
Psalm 24:3-4

Scholars believe that Psalm 24 represents the ceremony of the procession of the *King of Glory* through the Gates to His Seat in *the Most Holy Place.* This Last-Day Temple will be without spot or wrinkle, as this will be the one that opens the ancient gates to receive the *King of Glory* at His return. For God's Power to be released in fullness, on both an individual and corporate level, the structure must therefore be *'true to Plumb,'* a full and accurate representation of *the Christ.*

The span of the Temple of God is *the Son of God at its inception*—embedded in the foundation and pattern of Israel, it rises to the *Son of Man on the Cross,* at the crossroads of *His story.* Here, Agape love is extended to all who, by faith, belong to Him— those who came *before* and those who would come *after.* The span at its height is marked by *the Son of God at the end*—His Body reigning in Glory with Him, filled with the fullness of the Godhead. Its conclusion is marked by the emergence of the Headstone generation of the House of God, destined to be completed and revealed in the full union of the saints with Christ who is *the Head Stone (Eph. 4:13-16).*

This Final Stone is *Deity* in full union with His people, through which a Mighty Warrior emerges—*God's* ultimate *endgame.* Jesus was at the beginning, and He stands victorious in Majesty at the end in a perfected people. He is both the Alpha and the Omega, *"the Root and the Offspring of David..."* (Rev. 22:16).

"I am the Alpha and the Omega, the Beginning and the End," *says the Lord, "who is and who was and who is to come, the Almighty." Revelation 1:8*

We find ourselves now on the concluding page of His-Story, where the need for unity amongst apostolic leaders has become paramount to construct the seventh and final structure—*the Most Holy Place*, the Holy Habitation of the Lord.

God is presently orchestrating a grand mobilization of those who choose to willingly join forces with Him in the construction of His transcendent last-day Temple. These are individuals who possess ears finely attuned to His call. They are characterized by willingness and obedience, and a readiness to embrace the Cross and follow Him. They are committed to relinquishing all personal attachments and have wholeheartedly embraced Israel. God is summoning forth these builders—His apostles, prophets, teachers, evangelists, pastors, and an impassioned apostolic army—to carry out this work.

The House of God is designed in transcendence and is continually being brought into existence by Creator God—the Architect of the universe. He is omniscient, and omnipotent, the fountainhead of all wisdom, and epitomizes the profound and Divine nature of the House that is being built. The fear of *this God* is the beginning of wisdom!

The hastening of the Day of our Lord's return necessitates the agreement of His leadership with His work of the dismantling, remodeling, and restoration of His House, to conform it to the original Blueprint crafted by the Chief Architect.

THE RESTORATION OF THE KINGDOM TO ISRAEL

The work to build the end-time Temple of God is timed to begin in the season of preparation for the restoration of the *Kingdom to Israel*. There is much revelation to be mined from Acts 3:19-21, that brings insight and understanding into God's unfolding plan for the preparations required in the season of His return.

"Repent therefore and be converted, that your sins may be blotted out, so that times of refreshing may come from the presence of the Lord and that He may send Jesus Christ who

was preached to you before, whom heaven must receive ..." Acts 3:19

The Greek word *converted* in this scripture is *epistrophe* which means to *revert* or to *return*. The word refreshing is *anapsuxis* and means *the recovery of breath* or *revival*. Peter, addressing the gathered people of Israel, admonished them for causing the death of the Messiah. Despite their ignorance, he urged them to repent. He promised that the process of repentance would produce *opportune moments* (kairos times) that would release times of refreshing and a revival of the manifest Presence of the Lord Jesus through the Holy Spirit.

Heaven has *received Jesus* until the time ordained by the Father when He is released to *return*. This was told to the disciples on the Mount of Olives just before Jesus' ascension. At that time they asked Him the significant question of *whether it was the appointed time for the Kingdom to be restored to Israel*. He answered:

> *"It is not for you to know the times or dates the Father has set by his own authority" Acts 1:6*

Jesus did not rebuke the disciples for their question or imply that they were mistaken in their thinking. Instead, He infused their inquiry with hope for the future. He then entrusted them with the mission to spread the Gospel to the nations *during the interim period* before His return to restore all things and establish His Kingdom's reign from Jerusalem.

> *"...until the times of restoration of all things, which God has spoken by the mouth of all His holy prophets since the world began." Acts 3:20-21*

The *times* spoken of here are *chronos* times representing a *period* in history that was to come. The word for *restoration* is the Greek word *apokatastasis* and means *reconstitution and restitution, renewal, revival, or reestablishment, to reconstruct or return something to a former, original, normal, or unimpaired condition!*

What was in Peter's mind when he addressed Israel about the *restoration of all things* in this passage? This discourse occurred shortly after the birth of the Church in Jerusalem on the *Day of Pentecost,* making it unlikely that he was referring to the Church in the context of restoration. While two thousand years later, we might consider the Church in this context, Peter seems to be alluding to a different occurrence of transcendent significance— *the restoration of the Kingdom to Israel, "...which God has spoken by the mouth of His holy prophets since the worlds began."* (Remember the disciples had just a short time previously asked Jesus when would the Kingdom be restored to Israel).

Peter, along with all the apostles and the entirety of Israel, held the shared understanding that in a future era, the Kingdom of God over Israel, reminiscent of the days when David reigned, would be restored, and reinstated as foretold by the prophets. In this restored Kingdom, Jesus, the Son of David, was prophesied and destined to rule.

> *"David My servant shall be king over them, and they shall all have one shepherd; they shall also walk in My judgments and observe My statutes, and do them. Then they shall dwell in the land that I have given to Jacob My servant, where your fathers dwelt; and they shall dwell there, they, their children, and their children's children, forever; and My servant David shall be their prince forever." Ezekiel 37:24-25*

Israel has endured occupation since the loss of its kingdom and the destruction of the Temple by the Babylonians on the 9th of Av in 586 BC. However, in 1948—thousands of years later, through a historic and momentous United Nations vote, Israel was Divinely restored by God and given independence. The year 1948 marked the prophetic *initiation* of what Peter termed the *restoration of all things.* Currently, Heaven stands ready to usher

Jesus, the King of Glory to His Throne in Jerusalem. From here He will reign having dominion as Sovereign Lord over the entire world.

David's kingdom stood as the pinnacle of Israel's glory in its time. Fueled by an immense love for God, David harbored a deep, profound longing to construct a *Resting Place* for the Divine Presence. God, therefore, bestowed upon him both the design and abundant provisions for its construction. The temple that his son Solomon eventually built was a testament to David's devotion and God's favor.

"...the plans for all that he had by the Spirit..." "All this," said David, "the LORD made me understand in writing, by His hand upon me, all the works of these plans." 1 Chronicles 28:12, 19

King David was a man after God's heart as a representation of Christ the King of kings.

"In that day the LORD will defend the inhabitants of Jerusalem; the one who is feeble among them in that day shall be like David, and the house of David shall be like God, like the Angel of the LORD before them. It shall be in that day that I will seek to destroy all the nations that come against Jerusalem." Zechariah 12:8-9

Heaven holds and restrains Jesus in anticipation of the greatest event of all History—*the return of Christ to rule and reign on earth from Jerusalem.* Until then, we will have times of refreshing and revival all over the earth, with the manifest Presence of the Lord ever-increasing in greater and greater measure until He returns.

In British chronicles, another definition for the word restoration is *the re-establishment of a monarch.* We have presently entered the times of the *restoration of the Monarchy to Israel* in preparation for Christ our King's return to earth. The Lord along with the heavenly hosts and His apostolic leadership is beginning the work to restore His Temple.

'All things' must be restored to the Architect's original pattern of the Temple. Israel's place is a key feature in the structure of the Blueprint of God's design. Israel holds a strategic position in the centrality of God's administration and rule over the Earth. The importance of building on the unshakable foundation of Jesus Christ and the pattern He has ordained—which includes Israel, is underscored in Scripture.

"They serve at a sanctuary that is a copy and shadow of what is in heaven. This is why Moses was warned when he was about to build the tabernacle: "See to it that you make everything according to the pattern shown you on the mountain." Hebrews 8:5 (see also Rom. 11 and Ephes 2)

How and what we build upon this foundation matters: whether with gold, silver, precious stones, or with wood, hay, or straw, we will give an account. On that Day, each one's work will be tested by fire and the authenticity of our efforts will be exposed.

"According to the grace of God which was given to me, as a wise master builder I have laid the foundation, and another builds on it. But let each one take heed how he builds on it. For no other foundation can anyone lay than that which is laid, which is Jesus Christ. Now if anyone builds on this foundation with gold, silver, precious stones, wood, hay, straw, each one's work will become clear; for the Day will declare it, because it will be revealed by fire; and the fire will test each one's work, of what sort it is. If anyone's work which he has built on it endures, he will receive a reward. If anyone's work is burned, he will suffer loss; but he himself will be saved, yet so as through fire. Do you not know that you are the temple of God and that the Spirit of God dwells in you?" 1 Corinthians 3:10-16

This period of transition may resemble the time when Saul remained king even after he was rejected by God, highlighting God's permissible will until the appointed time comes.

The current times now call for a profound shift towards reformation, accompanied by great awakening and revival. Existing structures will have the choice to adapt to these transformative winds or be dismantled. Carnal works will inevitably be consumed in the refining Fire of transforming in an end-time season. It is only a matter of God's timing before *the Day* reveals the true heart motivation and nature of what has been built.

_____

_____

_____

_____

_____

_____

_____

Chapter Thirteen

IT SHALL BE HOLY!

"For we know in part and we prophesy in part. But when that which is perfect is come, then that which is in part will be done away. When I was a child, I spoke as a child I understood as a child, I thought as a child; but when I became a man, I put away childish things. For now we see in a mirror, dimly, but then face to face. Now I know in part but then I shall know just as I am known."
1Corinthians 13:9-12

Many years ago, I experienced a night that I can only describe as a most holy night. An appropriate description as the speaker was Sergio Scataglini who wrote the book, *"Fire of His Holiness."* The occasion was his very first visit to Catch the Fire Church and the first time he would speak there. Just before he was about to speak, the Lord brought back to his memory three words he had spoken in a conversation with some other leaders a few years prior. It was around the time when the outpouring first started, and he was in a meeting with some leaders who were discussing it. He knew nothing about it and was simply listening as they criticized what was occurring there. His only contribution to the conversation was the comment, *"That is not good."* For those three words, the conviction of the Holy Spirit fell upon him that night.

As he had already been in Toronto for a few days and had ample opportunity to apologize to John and Carol Arnott, the Founders, he asked the Lord why He was being reminded of this incident a few minutes before he was to speak. It turned out it was

131

the Lord's plan for him to repent *publicly* as He intended to do a deep work that night in rooting out the *sin of arrogance*. Conviction was so great upon him, that he was convicted about even standing on the platform. He explained to everyone what the Lord was saying and repented before everyone.

There were well over a thousand people there and the conviction of God fell on everyone. As he made the altar call for leaders to also repent, it seemed that almost everyone went forward. Waves of weeping and repentance swept through the night. The message that came through very clearly was that God was preparing to move, and for any who would follow, this sin had to be rooted out.

Those who will work with God to prepare the Most Holy Place are called to be holy, as He is Holy. Their hands must be free from bloodshed—*spiritual violence against other churches and servants of God.*

A PREPONDERANCE OF ARROGANCE

During a time of introspection, while examining my own heart regarding arrogance and reflecting on the pervasive arrogance within the Church, the Lord impressed upon my spirit the words *a preponderance of arrogance.* Drawing parallels with the case of Saul, whose kingship was forfeited due to pride, I understood that this trait must give way to a spirit of humility and brokenness. It is only through such humility that God's intended purposes can unfold through His apostolic leadership.

The attitude that asserts possession of full revelation, while dismissing from others, represents a prideful way that displeases God. Haughtiness must be replaced by a posture of humility and willingness to yield; this allows for a corporate spirit that aligns with the Divine will.

"For where envy and self-seeking exist, confusion and every evil thing are there. But the wisdom that is from above is first pure,

then peaceable, gentle, willing to yield, full of mercy and good fruits, without partiality and without hypocrisy." James 3:17

"This is the one I esteem: he who is humble and contrite and humble in spirit, and trembles at my word." Isaiah 66:2 NIV

Those who tremble at God's Word will have a Godly fear of also attempting to control anything in His House. Control can wear many faces and be very subtle. It will hide itself under the guise of good intentions and false humility. Control can achieve its aim by laying guilt on others to achieve its aim. Guilt is never used by the Holy Spirit in His work of sanctification.

Leaders may face the pitfall of succumbing to control when driven by the earnest desire to witness the best emerge from those within their sphere of guidance. This trap can be avoided when the brilliance of Christ is *shown* as the inspiration for others to follow. God's transformative work is then entrusted to the Holy Spirit where His guidance is allowed to take precedence. In doing so, leaders can create an environment where the potential of each individual is encouraged to flourish, free from the constraints of excessive control and manipulation.

ESTABLISH THE COVER

I once had a vision of the cartoon character, *the big bad wolf.* He was huffing and puffing, gathering up all the wind He could muster to blow upon the houses of the three pigs. In this, the Lord revealed that He was about to blow the roofs off some churches. I understood that God was going to allow the wolf to blow on houses built with religion and legalism—*the wood and the hay* (1 Cor. 3:12). Even though the wolf was not able to blow down the third house because it was built with solid brick, he was able to gain entry through an opening *in the roof,* but with wisdom, a strategy was executed to put an end to the wolf.

The Lord revealed the connection between roofs and governance as *the covering provided by His appointed leadership.*

The fullness of Deity God intends for the Headstone generation of apostolic leaders is designed to be a powerful transcendent covering for the Body of Christ—a powerful defense against the enemy's assaults. We are coming into a time on earth when it will be critical for sound apostolic covering to be secured in place as an anchor for the times.

When there is a warning of an impending storm, we prepare and take cover in a safe place. During a tornado, the safest place is to be secured to something that is firmly secured. It is important to prepare now for future storms by finding shelter under a sound leadership covering that is firmly anchored to Christ. The trumpet is beginning to sound the words loudly: *"Run for cover!"*

Leaders like David, Moses, Joseph, Samuel, and Deborah are after God's Heart as they most resemble the Master in their willingness to forgive completely and their desire to serve in wholeheartedness. The burden of the Lord is now to see His builders come together in unity to undertake the glorious task of completing the Temple. The job comes with an incredibly high price; great honor is therefore bestowed upon those who have the call to work with Christ to close this chapter of history.

GOD'S MEASUREMENT OF SUCCESS

In the Kingdom of God, His measurement of success is far different from the world standards. It must become clear that everything the Church has received was given by God—everything came from His hand. His measure of the success of each person, ministry, or church is therefore determined solely by *what He has given, and how well it has been used.*

A ministry or church might project an image of having great power, anointing, and success, yet they may have only tapped into a fraction of the Divine resources bestowed upon them by God, functioning from human ingenuity rather than submission to God. Conversely, another church or ministry may appear to be struggling and in continual warfare yet in obedience, utilizing every divine gift at its disposal. According to God's Divine standards, the seemingly struggling church is far more successful and triumphant.

A church may also thrive by fully employing the abundant provisions God has provided, but it is essential to recognize that no one can stand before God and boast about their accomplishments. All things become *equalized* in that all things originate from God, from our ability to breathe and most certainly our ability to build successfully.

> *"Yours, O Lord, is the greatness and the power and the glory and the majesty and splendor, for everything in heaven and earth is yours.... Everything comes from you and we have given you only what comes from your hand...O Lord our God, as for all this abundance that we have provided for building you a temple for your Holy Name, it comes from your hand, and all of it belongs to you." 1Chronicles 29:11-16 NIV*

This scripture underscores the profound truth that every leader devoted to serving the Lord wholeheartedly, irrespective of the size or significance of their tribe, the magnitude of anointing in their church, or its perceived strength or weakness, *success is measured always by eternal value.* From the most prominent and powerful to the smallest and seemingly weakest, the Holy Spirit is the great *Equalizer.*

When the Body has died a corporate death on the Cross, it will be transformed without *spot or wrinkle*, and rise in resurrection Power to meet Christ in the air. The Lord is sounding a trumpet across the Earth, sending out a message to His people that it is now time to rebuild Zion.

> *"You will arise and have compassion on Zion; for it is time to show favor to her, for the appointed time has come. For her stones are dear to your servants; her very dust moves them to pity. The nations shall fear the name of the LORD, all the kings*

of the earth will revere your glory. For the Lord will rebuild Zion and appear in his glory." Psalm 102:13-16 NIV

The altar of God's last-day Temple cannot be built or dedicated outside of *union with Israel.* God is calling for every builder of this Temple, to begin by coming together to build and dedicate the Altar to the Lord in unity, *and* in union of heart with Israel. It must be dedicated with all that He has given, that has *come from His hands*—churches, ministries, revelations, wealth, children, husbands, wives, possessions, houses, lands, cars, friends, faith, obedience, humility, and brokenness—*even life itself.*

As Israel makes its way back to the Land, the Spiritual Body of Jeshua is returning to Jerusalem in a union of heart with Israel to build the last Temple. God is sounding the word to return: *Return to the Land, return to Jerusalem, Return to your position before My Throne. Return to My Mind, My Heart, and My Thought. Gather before Me as One Man in Jerusalem the place of My heart!*

Israel went in to take the Promised Land as *one man.* All the dissent, division, complacency, grumbling, and rebellion had ended after being in the crucible of the wilderness years. God finally had a prepared people who would choose obedience to His will, and choose to work together. *Arrogance was left on the other side of the Jordan River.*

The Body of Christ must now also come ready to lay down all prejudices and the arrogance of *religion* and religious pride keeping the Church buried deep in hypocrisy and anchored firmly to the natural. As we let go of these heavy weights, to embrace true worship and reverence of a Holy God, the Church will begin to rise in Resurrection Power, into higher dimensions of Christ's Glory than it has ever known.

Out of the ashes of this sacrificial offering will come the resurrection of something so glorious and magnificent that the entire world will stop to take notice. In the Day of His Power, the enemies of God will tremble with fear at the revelation of these *sons of God* and the sound of the armies of the *Israel of God* marching together in unity to take back the Land. As these sons of God arise to take their place free of the mindsets of the past, having surrendered all to the Cross—all preconceived ideas and opinions of what church should look like, they will begin to work with the Master Builder to erect 'The Christ'—*the Model Church for the future.*

God is now preparing something authentic for the Climax of the Age through which the wolf will not be able to gain entry. The apostolic prophetic vanguard is comprised of leaders who will build to prepare an Ark as protection from the end-time storms and to contain the Harvest. To accomplish this feat, the Body desperately needs the Power, the Wine, and the Anointing of God. This precious River flows from the Throne of God *from the Most Holy Place*. When this Place has been prepared, the River of God will begin to flow in Fullness and Power to the Earth.

> *"Then he brought me back to the door of the temple; and there was water, flowing from under the threshold of the temple toward the east..." Ezekiel 47:1*

> *"And he showed me a pure river of water of life, clear as crystal, proceeding from the throne of God, and of the Lamb." Revelation 22:1*

THE BUILDERS

"According to the grace of God which was given to me,

as a wise master builder I have laid the foundation,

and another builds on it.

But let each one take heed how he builds on it."

1 Corinthians 3:10

Chapter Fourteen

FIVE-FOLD LEADERS

"And God has appointed these in the church: first apostles, second prophets, third teachers, after that miracles, then gifts of healings, helps, administrations, varieties of tongues. Are all apostles? Are all prophets? Are all teachers? Are all workers of miracles? Do all have gifts of healings? Do all speak with tongues? Do all interpret?"
1Corinthians 12:29

The building of the Headstone is the burden of the hour. This section is therefore dedicated to a thorough understanding of the vessels—the men and women whom God will use to shape it.

When men collaborated in unity to build the tower of Babel apart from God's will, in their goal to reach the heavens, *and their desire not to be scattered*, they stepped out onto extremely dangerous ground (Gen. 11:4). Cloaked in arrogance and operating from the sin of presumption, they attempted this project outside of the will of God, the direction of God and the purposes of God. Their intended aim became their sentence—*God scattered these builders across the face of the earth and confused their language*.

The builders of the church of earlier times fell into the same trap that worked to catapult them into the Dark Ages—a time when the Glory of God had departed. In arrogance and presumption, they began to build an empire modeled after their design, to make *for themselves* a name. They suffered the same sentence as a consequence. God came down and scattered their efforts across the face of the earth and confused their language and structures. The consequences are evident today in that in every nation, we have builders of thousands of denominations. Ingrained within each are their own semantics and 'religious' culture—every language tainted with a measure of spiritual pride. Though God was responsible for the initial birthing of many, most would ultimately fall into the trap of crystalized formalized, organized religion.

The timing of God is an important and very necessary ingredient to the building of the House of God as Spiritual precept is built upon precept. Time is vital to the Body's growth in wisdom and understanding and to the process of its healing and cleansing. Over time, as strongholds and demonic mindsets are demolished, God fills those areas with the *fullness* of His Life as the Body grows up toward the Head.

We are now approaching the end of the age, the time for the completion of the House of God, to emerge in the stature of Christ, to the Throne of God. Because of this, an incredible work led by the Lord is presently underway to invite the builders of His House to be re-gathered, *to build the Lord's way, and* to restore the House of God to the pure and undefiled language of submission and humility in the Spirit of Christ. This is a movement characterized by honor, a virtue necessary to build a Temple whose *'reach'* is Heaven and whose purity of heart touches the Throne of God—*as the pure in heart see God.* There is a movement toward union now underway to reverse *the scattering.*

The last day Temple of the *Most Holy Place* has room for only one Architect, one Master builder, one Archbishop, one Potentate, one King, and one Lord of all—*the Lord Jesus Christ, the Son of God.* Having given all for their King, His *servant leaders* are birthed as a holy sacrifice unto the Lord—the holy ground upon which He will stand to build and complete *His work.* God is preparing an army of builders, apostles, prophets, teachers, and pastors, of this caliber who will work with Him and *choose to work together* in unity, to finish His work.

This *Most Holy Place* will be built by mostly nameless, faceless servants, who choose to walk the way of the Cross and who will give their lives to bring forth His will in this dispensation. They will lay down every idol, including the unhealthy devotion to formulas, laws, regulations, financial gain, and obsessions with carnal patterns. They will walk away from all works of the flesh in radical obedience and radical passion, to embrace life led by the Spirit on a much higher plane. It is time to take the risk, to take the jump off the mountain of religion, personal agendas, and performance, and begin to soar in the Spirit as *He works* to complete the will of God.

> *"And he made known to us the mystery of his will according to his good pleasure, which he purposed in Christ, to be put into effect when the times will have reached their fulfilment—to bring all things in heaven and on earth together under one head, even Christ." Ephesians 1:9 NIV*

The five-fold apostolic ministry is purposed by Divine design, to work in partnership with God in the oversight of constructing His House according to His Blueprint. This model is illustrated in Scripture through the apostolic/prophetic team God assembled for the construction of the second Temple, which included Nehemiah, Ezra, Haggai, Zechariah, and Zerubbabel.

When the Jews returned to Jerusalem after the Babylonian captivity, all five leaders were given a significant part in God's work of restoration. Nehemiah and Ezra were instrumental in the reconstruction of Jerusalem—Nehemiah focused on rebuilding the walls, and Ezra was the teacher of *spiritual* restoration through the teaching of the Word. As King, Zerubbabel oversaw all efforts to rebuild the Temple and the city.

Haggai and Zechariah were the prophetic voices who prophesied during this time providing spiritual guidance and divine insight into God's heart for His House. They encouraged the people to stay the course. Ezra and Nehemiah also played roles in restoring worship and reestablishing the people's commitment to God. All were committed to the restoration of God's covenant with His people and the revival of their devotion to Him.

The present five-fold apostolic/prophetic company of leaders has been prepared through trials and tribulation under duress and incredible stress for an end-time ministry, to stand, and lead under extremely challenging and demanding situations. They are intended by God to be a Body of warrior leaders—a *Body prepared for Him,* to complete the Divine Will and Destiny on earth. These are the builders who will build with the sword of God in one hand and the power of God in the other. They work together to bring the worldwide Body of Christ (those with ears to hear and a heart to submit), into the union of *one Wineskin,* and oversee the entrance of the great Harvest into this Body.

Who are these men and women that comprise this great army of God's generals? These builders will be men and women from every walk of life, every tribe and tongue, and various streams in the Church. Why have they been chosen? We can only answer that question if we can answer why the twelve disciples were chosen, why Paul was chosen, or why Mary was chosen as the body that would carry the Savior of the world. The one characteristic these leaders all bear is their willingness to be obedient to the point of death, *in the likeness of their Master.*

Some say that leaders are born while others may say they are made. But leaders in God's Kingdom are neither. They are re-born, birthed in the desert places alone with God in the Crucible of His Love. Here they are fired, hammered, and beaten like gold into conformity and union with Christ, the Leader of all leaders. True leadership is born out of union with Christ. Anointed effective leadership, having the power to fulfill God's purposes for the end-times, is directly related to the quality of time spent with the Lord, sitting in His Presence, being immersed in His Life.

God's leaders are birthed out of the death experience in desert places where He takes His leaders to die. There in the process of their death, they become holy ground to the Lord—a prepared body for Christ. They return from the desert in the power of the Spirit with Christ sitting on the throne of their lives as *He* then steps forward to accomplish His ends. Christ is the only Leader capable of completing His Temple and leading His people into the Promised Land—the Kingdom of God.

Leadership is not learning methods, techniques, or patterns, it is becoming united to Christ Jesus, *our Divine Leader who is the Pattern*, who has His methods and ways of leading, tailored to each work. In times past and present, many anointed men have put in the time with the Lord and have come away with powerful leadership skills and strategies. These men and women went on to preach sermons and write books about what God had taught them in their wilderness years. Other leaders read these books or went to the seminars and conferences that taught the truths they learned, *without having put in the same quality of time with the Lord.* Consequently, they don't get the same results, as true anointed leadership begins with becoming one with Christ and His principles of leadership received directly from Him. The Lord's servants are conformed to Him in the fire of His Presence as they sit at His feet, loving and worshipping Him with fully surrendered hearts.

Moses, one of the greatest leaders in the Bible, trained to be a leader in Egypt, did not possess any leadership skills that were of value to God. God led him into the back of the desert to undo everything that he was to be made ready. David and John, the Baptist, two more great leaders, did not attend Leadership 101, or have any formal training that could have been of any benefit to them in the kingdom of God. One learned his lessons in the desert and the other in the pastures tending sheep in obscurity. These three men were each brought into conformity with the Lord during the years spent alone with Him.

The most important characteristic of leadership the desert produced in these men was humility and brokenness—*the only platform on which Christ can or will stand to lead His people.* The apostolic\prophetic platform of the end-times will be one fashioned after the Cross. Authentic apostolic/prophetic ministry will be recognized by the mantle of Christ's humility that covers it.

The apostolic is comprised of men and women marked by Christ. They bear His seal and will be recognized by the anointing, power, and humility. They will stand in all the authority of Christ and work to promote only *His* agenda to complete *His* purposes and fulfill *His* Destiny. They will keep Christ at the forefront of their ministry at all times. All that they do will point to Him, drawing others to Him, *not to themselves,* their churches, their methods, their patterns, or their agendas.

All that the apostles built and taught in the early church that has produced eternal fruit throughout the centuries was not firstly about methods or patterns, but by always pointing to Christ. Man's agenda is not going to build the Temple of *the Christ.* Leadership training that does not continually point back to Christ to give Him first place will be ineffectual at best and demonic at worst. Distraction and pulling away from the Plumb Line, even ever so slightly, is Satan's greatest weapon against God's work. Leaders must give Christ His sovereign place at all times as Lord of All.

Paul often referred to Himself as a prisoner of the Lord. He was one of God's most effective servants having died to all that the world had to offer while allowing Christ to confine him within Himself, in the prison of His love. Paul wrote often about the benefits of being *in Christ*, this is chiefly because he was writing from his home, his place of residence. It was a place that he knew very well, where he was very comfortable and at rest. From this place within Christ, he wrote his many epistles and his very transcendent letter to the Ephesians.

This letter written in an actual prison was born out of solitude with God. As Paul was sealed up alone with God in His Presence, the heavens opened to him. The narrowing of his life on earth led to the opening of the vast expanse of Heaven found in God's Presence. Paul's willingness to be reduced to nothing, provided God with a platform to become *everything,* and to maximize His output through Paul's life. Because of the quality of time, Paul spent with his Lord, the Life of Christ has continued to flow through His life for over two thousand years to this present day.

Many leaders may be operating at maximum capacity while Christ's influence through them remains minimal. This dynamic must be reversed, and transformation can only occur within the crucible of His Presence and love. Christ is the beginning and the end of a Christian's life and is the beginning and conclusion of true leadership.

When this Divine order is reinstated within the Body of Christ, the outflow of His life will increase. An outpouring of the anointed Power of God will emanate through His Body, possessing the *dunamis* power to impact the entire world. God desires to re-release this Power from His House and increase the sphere of its impact for the *summing up of all things.* For this to occur, leadership entrusted with the affairs of God must acknowledge His place as Supreme Ruler over all things, as the early apostles did.

Chapter Fifteen

APOSTLES & PROPHETS

"For we are co-workers in God's service; you are God's field, God's building. By the grace God has given me, I laid a foundation as a wise builder, and someone else is building on it. But each one should build with care. For no one can lay any foundation other than the one already laid, which is Jesus Christ. If anyone builds on this foundation using gold, silver, costly stones, wood, hay or straw, their work will be shown for what it is, because the Day will bring it to light. It will be revealed with fire, and the fire will test the quality of each person's work. If what has been built survives, the builder will receive a reward. If it is burned up, the builder will suffer loss but yet will be saved--even though only as one escaping through the flames."
1 Corinthians 3:9-15 NIV

Everyone is called to the work of building the House of the Lord, but God has His Divine order for the work to be carried out and has set certain ones in the Body to lead in certain functions of His work. God's intention is for the priesthood of all believers, as every believer is a potential leader. All believers should be encouraged and given every opportunity to grow and function in areas of leadership. However, potential leaders will possess not only the desire but also the willingness to cross over into a life of sacrifice and Holy fire—*the cost of true leadership.*

Nevertheless, certain leadership roles come only with the call of God, with specific assigned tasks in the work of gathering the lost, preparing the Bride of Christ, and building up the Body to the full measure of Christ. These are the apostle, the prophet, the evangelist, the teacher, and the pastor—fathers, and mothers overseeing the work and family of God (Eph. 4:11). These men and women have the call of *builder* on their lives—they gather, train, direct and oversee the work of building God's House to bring it to completion as a Bride prepared for Christ.

> *"It was He who gave some to be apostles, some to be prophets, some to be evangelists, and some to be pastors and teachers, to prepare God's people for works of service so that the body of Christ may be built up..." Ephesians 4:11 NIV*

The apostles and prophets not only laid the foundations of the House, but they also served foundationally as servants of the House. These leaders in union with Christ, together form the Headstone that completes the House and protects it as fathers and mothers. Together they form a *canopy of love* over the House. They are the fathers and the mothers of the *Family of God* anointed with wisdom to bring sons and daughters into maturity and an authentic unity that has its source in God.

At the end of the age, the Headstone generation of apostolic leaders will complete the House of God in union with Christ as the apostolic covering over it. This Headstone generation of leaders represents the shoulders of the Body upon which the Headship of Christ rests.

The Greek word *apostolos* is defined as *an ambassador of the gospel, a commissioner of Christ with miraculous powers, a sent one.* Jesus who was the first *Sent One* is the Apostle of the Faith. Those who have been sent by Christ enter a Holy union with Him for His purposes and are armed and equipped with His fullness as ones who are *Christ sent.*

To be truly *'sent'* or apostolic is to be *sent out from the Throne of heaven*, from the Heart of God. Sent ones are leaders who stand before the God of Heaven and are held accountable to Him. The one that is *sent* will in essence be possessed by the One *who has sent*. To be apostolic is to walk as Christ embodied in the fullness of His Deity. Paul could therefore say *"Imitate me, just as I also imitate Christ,"* to be apostolic is to be *Christ sent (1 Cor.11:1).*

This truth underscores the need to foster a close, voluntary relationship with apostolic fathers and mothers, whose genuine desire is not for control. Rather they work collaboratively in unity, dedicated to the profound goal of seeing Christ fully formed within those they serve. In doing so, individuals are equipped and released to fulfill their unique assignments. Authentic apostolicity will be recognized by its drive to *labor* or travail until Christ is formed in the communities they serve, within the sphere, He has given. The need for the restoration of apostles is essential to this hour, seeing that they are called to *complete* the work of Christ. They serve the Body to bring it into the fullness of the stature of Christ, for the work of ministry.

Authentic apostles and prophets have been gifted to identify the weaknesses and strengths of the Body of Christ in the local bodies they serve. They are equipped to bring the communities they serve into alignment with the Plumb Line of Jesus Christ. These *gifts of God* to the Body are anointed to speak God's word in power and direct the awesome task of bringing the Body into conformity and union with its Creator.

These leaders are *friends of the Bridegroom* sent to build and prepare the Bride *for the Bridegroom*. Like John the Baptist, they are sent to prepare His way. Those who do not receive the ones whom Christ has sent ahead of Himself, cannot therefore receive the gifts they have been sent to impart. These churches will be devoid of the anointing and the revelation needed to grow and fulfill their call to become the sanctuary prepared to receive Christ in His Glory. God always works through order.

> *"He who receives a prophet in the name of a prophet shall receive a prophet's reward. And he who receives a righteous man in the name of a righteous man shall receive a righteous man's reward." Matthew 10:41*

When the Temple is prepared according to God's Divine order, the Glory follows. *The measure that churches are aligned to the Plumb Line of Christ, His will and mandate for their house, is the* measure of Glory it will possess. Apostles and prophets are appointed and anointed with Christ's wisdom as builders in the work of building the Temple of God. They will work together as did Haggai, Zechariah, Joshua, and Zerubbabel in the rebuilding of God's Temple.

> "I am with you, says the LORD." So the LORD stirred up the spirit of Zerubbabel...governor of Judah, and the spirit of Joshua... the high priest, and the spirit of all the remnant of the people; and they came and worked on the house of the LORD of hosts, their God..." Haggai 1:12-15

With the leadership anointing of Jesus on them, leaders *become* the Plumb Line in union with Christ, ensuring that the measurements and the standard of the building are true to Plumb. In the book of Acts, we see the work of the building going up according to plan under the leadership of the apostles. Each level of the House goes up with significant revelation as precept is built upon precept.

As was stated in a previous chapter, Christianity began to lose the Glory of His Presence when it became established as the state religion of Rome in the third century. Over time it became entangled with Rome's government and degenerated even further. The Roman Empire established its own City of God, its hierarchy of priesthood, and its standards of righteousness. The consequence of disobedience to God's order and deviating from the written Word is that birth is given to something other than what God has intended. This in turn becomes a body deformed, and even grotesque when compared to the humility, beauty, simplicity, and majesty of Christ Jesus.

The Lord is now recovering and restoring authentic apostles and prophets to His Body to build the Headstone comprised of an apostolic army of servants. Over the past century, the Lord has restored the teacher, the pastor, and the evangelist to His Church. In the last five decades, we have seen the restoration of the prophetic and the emergence of prophets. God is now restoring to His Church its apostolic mandate as at first, for the work *to complete* the House of God.

Over the last forty years, there has been a great body of teaching released on the apostolic and the role of the apostle in the Body. This has been timed by God to coincide with the preparation of the end-time Temple for the return of Christ, as *only the authentic apostle and prophet* have the anointing to lead the work of completing the House of God according to the Architect's blueprint.

Apostles and prophets have been given an anointing to identify failing religious systems and deceptive practices founded on traditions—to tear down and destroy, to build and plant, and to bring restoration and order to God's House. As apostles laid the foundations, they will be given the wisdom and understanding to *complete it.*

> *"See, I have this day set you over the nations and over the kingdoms, to root out and to pull down, to destroy and to throw down, to build and to plant." Jeremiah 1:10*

Apostles and prophets have been gifted by God to both see and understand the larger comprehensive picture, to build from a global perspective and framework rather than only a local mindset. They find innovative ways to work together to facilitate the Body's movement toward union with Christ. God equips these leaders with the tools with which to navigate the Church through the host of challenges that are on the horizon and the storms that lie ahead.

Jesus came to Israel, to reveal the Father and the heart of the Father. He came to demolish a religion whose focus had become the rituals, ordinances, and pageantry, devoid of the love and compassion of God that comes only through an intimate relationship with the Father. Jesus came as the expressed image of God to give Israel a revelation of His love, and to tear down the religious structure that was keeping Israel bound and separated from the true knowledge and understanding of God.

Jesus' life was the new structure and Wineskin that was needed, one founded on the Love of the Father and *a radical departure from the old ways of religion.* He took the twelve through a period of discipleship training and at the appointed time, released them as apostles (sent ones) to begin the new work. These leaders were prepared and positioned by their obedience to *His instructions, for the move of the Holy Spirit that was about to occur.*

The Breath of the Holy Spirit brought Life into the structure. It produced a kingdom of priests who ministered *to God* and kings who would *serve His will* in the nations of the earth. These sweeping changes began to take effect as judgment fell on the religious structure of *stone* that was destroyed by the Romans in 70 A.D.

God is about to complete His final Resting Place—the temple that is the *Holy of Holies.* And as He did at His first coming, He will again root out and tear down all areas of dead religion— *religious ritual void of the life and love of God having an emphasis on man and man's agenda.* The Sanctuary being prepared for the Lord at His second coming will be equally as radical in comparison to what has so far been built over the past centuries. This *Most Holy Place* will be prepared as the present outer court religious structures begin to be dismantled, and the business of religious work in the Holy Place winds down.

The next great wave of the Holy Spirit will come at the appointed time to give birth to the Headstone as apostles again take their place and begin to function together in unity with the prophets, evangelists, pastors, and teachers. God will not send a harvest of billions of baby Christians into the Church to be eaten alive by religious, judgmental spirits, and much contention, strife, and division—*resulting in certain chaos.*

Apostles are anointed to bring order. They are being set in place as *fathers and mothers,* to train and equip other leaders, and bring them to full maturity for the overall protection of the sheep. This is essentially the anointing of Elijah, sent to prepare the way for the coming of the Lord.

The apostles and prophets—the builders who lay foundations are now being released for the work of summing up all things in Christ. Their job is to impart God's vision, provide direction, announce, and pronounce God's Word. They root out, pull down, build, and plant. They work with the Lord to see His Bride formed without spot or wrinkle.

> *"And God has appointed these in the church: first apostles, second prophets, third teachers..."* 1 Corinthians 12:28

Ephesians chapter four identifies the full scope of God's work in building His house from the foundation through to its completion in Glory. This chapter reveals God's plan and helps us to see and understand the specific purposes and fruit of leadership in the form of apostles, prophets, evangelists, pastors, and teachers.

These leaders have been ignited with the passion of Christ and have the anointing to release both passion and power into the congregation. Their job is to edify the Body (encourage and build up); to equip the saints for the work of ministry (discipleship); to protect by preventing deceptive doctrines from creeping into the Body; to facilitate the Body's growth into maturity; to release the gifts in the Body for every part to do its share; to bring the Body into the unity of the faith, and to facilitate and shape the body's growth into a perfect man, the measure of which *is Christ.* If these measures are in place, they will induce growth in the Body as it is built up in love.

Paul declared that the kingdom of God was not a matter of talk *but of power.* Apostolic leaders are now being prepared to release mighty demonstrations of His Power in the last days as at first.

"Truly the signs of an apostle were accomplished among you with all perseverance, in signs and wonders and mighty deeds" 2Corinthians 12:12

God is moving now to usher in something fresh, new, and vibrant, flowing in the Power of God. One that will perform exploits in the name of Jesus and does the *"greater things"* of releasing signs and wonders into the earth as in the times of Moses and Jesus. This move will bring a *restoration* of the foundational principles the Assembly of God is built on, *yet it will be new, as it is tailored specifically for the challenges of the end times and the dynamic of receiving Christ!*

The missionary mindset of plowing is being replaced with the apostolic mindset of power, authority, and success, which bear great fruit. The domineering leadership of an exalted pastor, or, of un-anointed religious elders (bishop or presbytery), is being transformed into vibrant teams of gifted anointed, apostolic servant leaders of the five-fold. These are men and women filled with the Holy Spirit and with power, functioning together alongside the main leader, under the covering of apostles and prophets. These apostolic teams together form the Headstone of the Temple of God and will usher in a manifestation of the Glory of God unique to the end of the age.

Nevertheless, there is a great danger in believing that a model can be put together by man's reasoning and believing it will produce Glory. It is possible to get everything right, have knowledge, wisdom, truth, and faith, have the right structure and the right people on the team, and yet still not have the Power and the Glory. How is this possible? The Glory embedded in the resurrection Power of God comes only via the *death experience*—a death that can only be accomplished *by the Holy Spirit* as we submit to this process. The Resurrection Power of the Holy Spirit was released through the suffering and death of Christ. The cry of those who form the Headstone with Christ must be that of Paul:

"But what things were gain to me, these I have counted loss for Christ. Yet indeed I also count all things loss for the excellence of the knowledge of Christ Jesus my LORD, for whom I have suffered the loss of all things, and count them as rubbish, that I may gain Christ and be found in Him, not having my own righteousness...that I may know Him and the power of His resurrection, and the fellowship of His sufferings, being conformed to His death, if by any means, I should attain to the resurrection from the dead." Philippians 3:7-11

The Lord helped me to understand that the *fellowship of His suffering* is not only the suffering that comes with the refining of the Holy Spirit, in the fire of His love, or even of enduring suffering as a servant on Christ's behalf. The *fellowship of His suffering* is intimately knowing Christ, becoming one with him in His purposes, and entering *His Passion*—the motivation behind His suffering, *the goal* of His suffering, *and the communion of His suffering.* We become one with Him in His magnificent obsession, the foundation of all His actions—*the bringing forth of His Bride in the summing up of all things within Himself.*

In becoming one with Christ, we are caught up in the current of *His passion*, His obsession becomes our obsession, His Destiny our destiny. When the Life of Christ in us occupies all and we are brought into full maturity and completion through the death process of picking up our cross daily, we enter union with Him through the power of His resurrection. We become joined to Him in His work—the fellowship, the Holy Communion of His suffering for the Church, His Body; being conformed to Him in His death and therefore also His Life.

The coming forth of the Headstone is the coming forth of an army of leaders in union with Christ, prepared to complete His purposes at the end of the age. They will be apostolic, bearing the burden of the nations, standing in apostolic resolution to the purposes of God, and moving in sync with Christ in all *apostolic patience.* They will be radical in their obedience to Christ, radical in their submission, radical in their passion for Christ, and radical in the *Passion of 'The Christ.'*

God will release His Power to complete His vision! There is a *"Day of Power"* coming when the preparation has been completed in leaders individually, and they become ready, prepared, and willing to build corporately.

"Your people shall be volunteers in the day of Your power; In the beauties of holiness, from the womb of the morning, You have the dew of Your youth." Psalm 110:3

Chapter Sixteen

THE DIVINE SCAFFOLD

"Whom will He teach knowledge? And whom will He make to understand the message? Those just weaned from milk? Those just drawn from the breasts? For precept must be upon precept, precept upon precept, line upon line, line upon line, here a little there a little." Isaiah 28:9-10

A scaffold is a *temporary* structure surrounding a building, erected, and used by builders in its construction or restoration. In education and learning, the word scaffold represents a method of teaching that assists students in understanding *new concepts and precepts*. With the apprehension of the precept, the scaffold support can then be gradually removed until it is no longer required.

Five-fold Apostolic leaders fashioned and fired in the precepts of the Word of God comprise *the scaffold God uses* to build His House. In this chapter, I would like to explore both definitions of scaffold: *precepts,* and *structure,* concerning the work of building *the Most Holy Place*—the end-time Sanctuary of God.

The path the saints travel, on the journey of being built up as a corporate house and rising as a Temple toward the Most Holy Place, is constructed of many scaffolds. Each is designed to keep us moving toward the Light, into greater revelation, expanded vision, and higher dimensions in Christ. We press on as Spiritual concepts are first apprehended to then become foundational. In the process, the believer is being consumed by God to perceive Christ in greater and greater measures of His Glory. A greater level of maturity is then achieved in conformity to Christ. To retain and maintain the impartations, revelations, and understanding gained, believers must become saturated in the measure of the Life of Christ revealed at each stage of the journey.

A scaffold acts as a springboard to every subsequent level, *or* a bridge to the *primary* goal, efficiently moving the disciple to the next level of learning. In the construction of buildings, the scaffold surrounds the building providing the workers with a safe position from which to work while providing access to the building. In some cases, the building is not seen until completion when the scaffolds are removed, and the structure is unveiled.

Another definition of scaffold is *a platform built on which men are put to death.* Each level of the scaffold we have been climbing on our journey over history, in the construction of the Temple of *'The Christ,'* on the ascent *to* Christ, *into* the Holy of Holies, has been designed by God to lead us through the crucifixion process. We arrive at the highest place—the very seat of God's throne, where only dead men can stand to declare:

> *"I have been crucified with Christ; it is no longer I who live, but Christ lives..." Galatians 2:20*

On arrival at this place, the pilgrim is consumed, immersed, and baptized into the structure of *'the Christ,'* as the scaffold that brought them to this *terrible* and Holy place is consumed under their feet. The believer's life then becomes the scaffold Christ uses to stand and release *His Life.*

The *apostolic\prophetic* platform is comprised of dead men walking. In the end, nothing is left standing other than *'The Christ.'* Every scaffold that led to this *Awesome* place will come down, fall away, and be destroyed! Everything is temporary until the *'Perfect'* makes His appearance; the scaffolds are then removed and the Heavenly structure is unveiled in His Glory. *Only what is found in Him remains!*

"But where there are prophecies, they will cease; where there are tongues, they will be stilled; where there is knowledge, it will pass away. For we know in part and we prophesy in part, but when perfection comes the imperfect disappears." 1 Corinthians 13:8-10

At Pentecost, the *apostolic/prophetic model* became the scaffold God used to lay the foundation of the superstructure of His House. It will also be the one He concludes with to build the Headstone. The lives of these men and women, and the fruit of their ministry, became the foundation of the walls, integrated into the foundation of the Temple laid in the prophets and apostles of Israel. The apostolic/prophetic model is a platform made up of an army of *dead sons and daughters* through whom Christ will complete His work at the end of the age.

The principle of the scaffold is one God has used to build His House. God has used many models of delivery to build Divine precept upon precept in the construction of His Temple. These temporary scaffolds such as Moses' Tabernacle, the Law, and the Prophets, were designed to move His people along a path or a timeline through many levels of Spiritual understanding. They were designed to move the people forward as they were able to grasp the fullness of the revelation or lessons being taught. God intends that His people make their arrival at the completion of His dream, the Primary—*the unveiling and full revelation of 'The Christ.'*

There are concepts in the Old Testament relating to God the Father, the Son, and the Holy Spirit that are foundational and eternal, while others such as the physical temple, its furnishings, the rituals, and the sacrifices, were a temporary scaffold model. These were designed to release a heavenly revelation, to teach and establish principles that would lead to a fuller revelation of the Temple, *which is Christ.* Upon arrival at the place of union and full integration with *The Christ,* all models and their method of delivery are no longer required. With an affinity for models and methods, this understanding is important for God's leadership to grasp. All models are inconsequential in the Presence of *the Christ*!

"We are reborn into a perfect inheritance that can never perish, never be defiled, and never diminish. It is promised and preserved forever in the heavenly realm for you! Through our faith, the mighty power of God constantly guards us until our full salvation is ready to be revealed in the last time. With our human tendency to lean toward methods, models, and patterns, this is important for us to grasp today." 1 Peter 1:4 TPT

MESSIAH - THE ARK OF GOD
THE HOUSE OF GOD

CHRIST
THE HEAD STONE

THE HEAD STONE
GENERATION

CORNERSTONE

FOUNDATION
STONE

Purposed by God, the authentic architectural design of the Temple is reflected in the Great journey of the pilgrim toward the fullness of life in His Presence and Glory. This Blueprint was established over history through various dispensations, using many scaffolds comprised of Divine precepts and concepts. Each scaffold was designed having one purpose—that the pilgrim be consumed into the very Substance of the Life of God. Although the model of each scaffold on the ascent to *the Christ* may have been temporary, relegated to its time, the eternal fruit each has wrought becomes foundational, embedded into the structure.

In the pride of man, builders can easily get distracted by the temporal to build elaborate structures. The Washington Monument is an example of this. It is said that the scaffolding built for this monument in earlier restorative work was such an eyesore that a prominent architect was hired to design another one more pleasing to the eye, costing millions of dollars. Many *preferred* the monument with the new *designer scaffolding* to the actual monument itself. What a revelation for those called the build the House of God that is *the Christ.*

Throughout history, God employed various denominations, ministries, and movements as scaffolds to construct His House. As with the example of the Washington Monument, many of the builders became fixated on the scaffolding rather than on the majesty, magnificence, and purity of the Temple of *The Christ.* Many have even attempted to design grander scaffolding structures than were intended by the Lord, embellished in the flesh by religion, pomp, and vainglory. Despite this, certain old scaffolds, originally designed as stepping stones, persist today, continuing to serve God's purposes, albeit in a very limited capacity.

It is important to learn from the past and seek to understand *the part* each has played in the overall framework of God's plans. Much can be learned from how past movements have served God's purposes as a model of delivery to move the Body onto higher levels of revelation for a subsequent season in time. Rather than looking back, it is important to look forward to Christ—*the Perfect*, as all models are flawed in some respect.

In the unfolding narrative of His story, we stand at the juncture where the corporate work to construct the final tier of the structure has become critical! In preparation for this final Wineskin, it is imperative to be released from the grip of past narratives, outdated models, and approaches. The time has come to embrace the full revelation—the *apocalypse of The Christ*. Each existing model must become aligned with Christ, to be integrated into the ultimate structure that will receive Him. As the Temple nears completion, all scaffolds and models will be discarded in the purifying fire of His approach—it is therefore pointless to make an idol out of churches, ministries, and denominations we have built. The House that receives Him is a House of worship and prayer for all nations.

> *"The quality of materials used by anyone building on this foundation will soon be made apparent, whether it has been built with gold, silver, and costly stones, or wood, hay, and straw. Their work will soon become evident, for the Day will make it clear, because it will be revealed by blazing fire! And the fire will test and prove the workmanship of each builder."* 1 Corinthians 3:12-13 TPT

The Body has been on a Divine and transcendent journey. The destination is the Holy of Holies, the place of the Presence—into full union with *The Christ*. In the end, Jesus Christ is all that will remain standing; everything outside of Him will fall away through the fires of Tribulation.

> *"Rise and measure the temple of God, the altar, and those who worship there. But leave out the court which is outside the temple, and do not measure it, for it has been given to the Gentiles. And they will tread the holy city underfoot for forty-two months."* Revelation 11:1-3

During Jesus' three years of ministry on Earth, He resorted to violence only twice, both times in the Outer Court of the Temple. He turned over the tables and brought out the whip in fierce anger that His Father's House had been turned into a den of robbers (Matt. 21:13). He quoted Jeremiah 7:11 who prophesied to Israel about impending judgment. Jeremiah cautioned Israel not to trust in deceptive words or the belief that they could continue in sin, falsely believing that God would not destroy His House saying, *"This is the Temple of the Lord"* *"...But go now to My place which was in Shiloh, where I set My name at the first, and see what I did to it..." (7:4,12).* That temple or model was judged by God and found wanting.

Just as the Temple of the *'law and the covenant'* did not insure Israel against judgment, the Temple and the Covenant of the Blood do not protect presumption, rebellion, and disobedience from the consequences of a Holy God who disciplines His children (Heb. 10:26). The Blood was sprinkled in the Holy Place and the Holy of Holies, *not in the Outer Court.* Whatever can be judged will be judged. Whatever can be shaken will be shaken. Whatever is carnal cannot enter eternity, The Outer Court is the carnal skin of the Body that must be shed.

> *"I know that my redeemer lives, and that in the end He will stand upon the earth. And after my skin has been destroyed, yet in my flesh I will see God." Job 19:25 NIV*

Some in the church today live from the Outer Court, preach from the Outer Court, and write books from the Outer Court. They have not concerned themselves with the need to press forward on the journey to the *Holy of Holies* to become intimately united with the Lord. God is presently using great trials and tribulation as the impetus to propel and push His people forward toward and into the Holy of Holies as protection from the coming storms.

In the end, Jesus will overturn the money tables and bring out His whip in the Outer Court to those who have made His Father's House a den of thieves. Those who have prophesied and done signs and wonders in His name for personal gain and glory have robbed God of His rightful place. To these, He will say, *"Depart from Me, I never knew you" (Matt. 7:23).*

The consequence of not moving on with God on His trajectory, to sum up all things, *is to fall behind.* God is sounding a loud trumpet of warning to get into the safe place of the Holy of Holies. He is prodding and pushing His people through trials, n a movement toward Glory. Many will choose not to commit and will stay settled in complacency and lukewarmness in an Outer Court scaffold doomed to destruction.

In the last days, God will allow those outside of the Holy of Holies to be refined in the fire of *great tribulation,* to be shaken free of deception into *His reality.* The Outer Court will be trampled but Outer Court dwellers will be saved, yet as by Fire (1 Cor. 3:15). The carnality of every model will be consumed by the Fire of God's Presence as He draws close for judgment, and the summing up of all things in His Son.

False apostles and prophets who have not been sent by God, prophesy peace and deceive those who follow the stubbornness of their hearts into believing that *"...no harm will come to you"* (Jer. 23:17).

God will judge and shake His church until sin is abandoned. God allowed Israel to be defeated at Shiloh, the Ark was taken by the enemy, the Glory departed and Eli the high priest died at the news of his son's death. This was all prophesied by Samuel because of the wickedness in the house of Eli (Sam. 3:11). Discipline will come to those who continue in rebellious sin, and trials to those who are lukewarm and complacent. The only place of safety in the storm is the *secret place of the Most High* where there is protection (Ps. 91).

Many people foolishly believe that God would not let His children suffer. God allowed His only beloved Son to suffer much in life and on the Cross, *"It was the Lord's will to crush him and cause him to suffer"* (Is. 53:10 NIV). Why would God allow this? Because He was seeing ahead to the fruit: that Christ, through His death would *"...justify many"* (v.11). This is the message of the Cross, and the reality of life for one who picks up his cross and walks the *Way of the Christ*—that out of death and suffering comes resurrection life, joy, and great fruit.

After a season of suffering, refining, and captivity in Babylon, God commissioned and sent His builders to return and rebuild the Temple. The builders, and the prophets, who prophesied throughout the work, were commissioned, and sent by God. This is presently occurring as God's apostolic/prophetic builders are being commissioned and sent out. God is about to build the last phase of His Temple that will tell the *last story* of history. The apostolic/prophetic model is the scaffolding *God* has designed to complete the work for Jesus' Return.

Chapter Seventeen

AUTHENTIC APOSTOLICITY

"I know your works, your labor, your patience, and that you cannot bear those who are evil. And you have tested those who say they are apostles and are not..." Revelation 2:2

Jesus cautioned His people not to be deceived; He warned that many false leaders would come in His name saying that *they are the Christ*. Some will come preaching *another Christ*, but they will be anti-Christ (Matt. 24:5, Mar. 13:6). The end of the age will be a time of great spiritual confusion as old religions merge, new religions appear, and demonic spirits invade the Church to bring division. Some leaders within the Church will fall into deception and begin to preach another Christ and another Gospel apart from what is established in the Word of God.

Authentic apostolic leaders, who are designated *friends of the Bridegroom,* are vital to the protection of the sheep, bringing forth the Bride of Christ and preserving God's interests on Earth. The Church must be equipped and taught to recognize the authentic leaders sent by God, to distinguish them from the multitude of counterfeits that will be released by the enemy to snatch the complacent, the lukewarm, and lead them into error.

"The harp and the strings, the tambourine and flute, and wine are in their feasts; but they do not regard the work of the LORD, nor consider the operation of His hands. Therefore my people have gone into captivity, because they have no knowledge..." Isaiah 5:14

A greater measure of wisdom and discernment will be needed in the last hour, a time when cold love and cunning deceptions will be predominant. God's people must pray for renewed minds having wisdom, as He has promised in His Word to give wisdom to those who ask for it. However, to fear the Lord is the beginning of wisdom, as His Word says (Prov. 9:10).

In this chapter, we will use the concept of the scaffold as shown in the previous chapter, in the process of proving the authenticity of the builders of the House of God.

Authentic apostolic scaffolding provides structure:

The idea and principle behind the scaffold is that each level of learning builds on the previous; each becoming increasingly more trying as we assimilate, progress, and pass the tests. This can be demonstrated in many aspects of life, for example, in education: from the process of learning in early childhood to the understanding of the complex concepts of higher learning in higher education.

Modeling is a method of instruction and support to the pilgrim on the journey as he learns new concepts and develops in understanding and gifting. Genuine apostolic scaffolding establishes the framework for the House of God, composed of living stones, on its ascent to maturity in the Head. Apostles and Prophets are the fathers and mothers who provide support and direction to the House through revelatory instruction from the Word of God and by modeling the truths they impart. Modeling is the most effective method for learning in the Kingdom—Jesus demonstrated this magnificently, and Paul declared *follow me as I follow Christ!*

The Word of God serves as the guiding path on the journey to Christlikeness, providing the building blocks for growth and ensuring the pilgrim stays on course. Clear boundaries anchored in the truth of Christ, create a secure platform for God's work and the freedom to learn while religious structures erode initiative, motivation, and the Presence of God.

Builders who work on the House of God must not confuse the scaffolding—their church, ministry, or leadership, *with the Temple of God.* The Temple that is the Christ and the living stones being built up in Him are the primary objects of attention—the scaffolding that He uses to build is *secondary.*

In the last days, the apostolic\prophetic scaffold, constructed by God will consist of diverse parts—a variety of church streams and Ministries that are distinct in purpose. The function is far more important than the form. In many cases, the functions of certain scaffolds may be identical, varying only in semantics, while others are designed quite differently by the Lord to fulfill specific purposes. In either case, the structure must be clearly defined and designed with checks and balances that keep the hungry soul persevering toward the intended goal without stifling the work of the Holy Spirit.

Authentic apostolic scaffolding is built for safety:

The apostolic/prophetic scaffold consists of leaders prepared and trained in God's refining fire. Having undergone this process, they gain a deep understanding of His ways. They are unfazed by earthly constraints and fearlessly embrace Godly risks. Completely devoted to God, they stand prepared to be a living sacrifice for Him. Liberated from worldly attachments and the fear of death, they possess an unwavering commitment to God alone. Their full allegiance to Christ designates them as secure places for Him and others.

Apostolic/prophetic scaffolding is carefully crafted for safety, serving as a secure platform for Christ to construct His Temple and fulfill His purposes while offering protection to His Body. Similar to constructing a building, assembling a scaffold at greater heights can be a challenge. Working at the highest levels demands stable, carefully assembled structures, not hastily put together, untested, or easily shaken. A mature apostolic/prophetic framework built together by strong relationships protects against these challenges. Such a structure becomes a barrier from the elements (demonic winds), at elevated heights and will become a safety net for completion of the work.

Joseph is a true example of the scaffold of apostolic leadership. His life revealed the process of training to reign with Christ. Joseph was sent ahead to preserve the lives of God's children and His purposes on earth, *"...God sent me before you to preserve life"* (Gen.45:5). The world of that time was greatly blessed through Joseph because of his willingness to remain faithful to the Lord through the crucible of preparation and testing.

David's reign also provides a prophetic picture of Christ's righteous reign as King over the Father's Kingdom and reflects the fruit of great leadership. His rule shows the beauty and fruit of leaders who lead in righteousness with Christ as *sons of God*. It is tremendous what God can accomplish on earth through one faithful and obedient servant—leaders like David who have His heart. An army of such leaders brought forth to complete the Lord's work will be awe-inspiring. The Word describes the majesty of such leadership as seen in David:

> *"The Spirit of the LORD spoke by me, And His word was on my tongue. The God of Israel said, the Rock of Israel spoke to me: 'He who rules over men must be just, Ruling in the fear of God. And he shall be like the light of the morning when the sun rises, A morning without clouds, Like the tender grass springing out of the earth, By clear shining after rain."* 2 Samuel 23:2-4

Authentic apostolic\prophetic scaffolding defines purpose and delivers clear direction:

The Apostolic/prophetic model distinctly articulates and illuminates God's purpose with a focused, heavenly vision. This model imparts clear revelation of God's intent and will, at both micro and macro levels, offering a Divinely crafted roadmap toward the fulfillment of the revelation.

In the last days, the apostolic/prophetic model must embody the entirety of God's vision and counsel, rather than focusing solely on specific aspects of Christ. As ambassadors of Christ, they will represent the completeness of Christ—His obedience, humility, love, power, anointing, wisdom, and understanding, and *His Hebraic roots*. Moreover, as ambassadors, they embrace the diversity present in *the Christ*—reaching out globally to the world Christ died for. They acknowledge and honor the diverse composition of the Body He is building, encompassing Jew and Gentile, male and female, and all societal classes and cultures.

Over the centuries we have observed the Temple of Christ *in parts* as understanding has been *in part*. In building and completing the Headstone Sanctuary, it is important to now build with a vision of the *whole*, with the focus and standard on *the fullness of the stature of Christ*. Leaders can no longer function from obedience *in part* but from *complete obedience* (2 Cor. 10:6). This requires that the humility of leaders be made complete. Those who have traversed the journey and carry the mantle of leadership must guide those still finding their way. They direct their communities toward the ultimate prize, which is Christlikeness, attained through a life of *Christ-like obedience*.

Establishing boundaries is an essential factor for maintaining order within the House of God. The law, now inscribed on our hearts, serves as a training tool, enabling the pilgrim to live and soar in the Spirit. When this perspective is lost, and the focus shifts solely to rule-keeping, this restricts the ability to soar in the Spirit and rise beyond the constraints of the law. Saints may then resist or settle instead of persisting on the journey of ascension in Christ.

In this pivotal moment, as we approach the culmination of the age, stagnation is a luxury we cannot afford. Our journey must persist unwaveringly in the direction of the Ark of Christ. Given that leaders carry the responsibility of bearing the Ark, it is imperative for them to inspire others by exemplifying a steadfastness that motivates the saints to press forward. People naturally emulate their leaders, and if leaders choose to settle, others will likely follow suit.

The leadership of Joshua is an inspiration to all leaders. He served God in an exemplary fashion to prepare and guide the people to move corporately in alignment with God's directions. He led them as a guide on the transcendent journey with the *Lord of Hosts* towards possession of the Promised Land.

> *"Prepare provisions for yourselves, for within three days you will cross over this Jordan, to go in to possess the Land which the Lord your God is giving you to possess." Joshua 1:1*

It is important now to keep our eyes fixed on the Ark and the authentic leaders who carry it on this last leg of the journey, *as we have not been this way before.* In the book *'Moses'* written by Chuck Swindoll, he describes the early part of our journey with God by comparing it to a young untrained dog who continually pulls on his leash in frustration, choking, and breathing heavily, while dragging his master around. I was very convicted as I saw myself in that picture in my early walk with God. I saw my impatience, frustration, and despair, always trying to get God to move a little faster, to do what I wanted. The problem was, after years of fire and hammering, I now felt more like the old, tired dog that only wanted to lie down, whose master was continually yanking his chain to get him moving. At that time, I was very weary, I believe Isaiah 37:3 described my condition and maybe the condition of many in the Body today.

> *"...for the children have come to the time of birth, but there is no strength to bring them forth." Isaiah 37:3*

Twenty-five years ago, as I was walking to the bus stop one morning to go to work, I saw my bus waiting at the stop while I was a distance away. I began to walk faster. I didn't think I would make it and prayed to the Lord to hold the bus for me. As I prayed, I sensed that He was going to hold it, but at the same time, the thought entered my head that I could not afford to slacken my pace as the bus driver had a schedule to keep. At that moment, I realized that the Lord was speaking to me.

After years of preparation, training, and intense Fire, the Body of Christ cannot afford to settle down or slacken its pace. The Lord is getting ready to move. He has been holding the Bus for us, but He does have a schedule to keep. That morning the thought of being left behind made me realize how much I wanted to be on the bus and it shook me out of the place of complacency I was falling into. The Ark is setting out and God has a schedule to keep! We must press on and keep moving and good leadership inspires the saints to do so.

An Authentic apostolic\prophetic scaffold will be built in union:

Authentic apostolic/prophetic scaffolding will choose to build together in unity to become a secure and safe platform for the Lord. God will assemble authentic apostolic councils comprised of five-fold leaders who say yes to Him and choose to build alongside each other. This is not something that man can put together—God alone makes the Divine connections. These councils birthed in the power of agreement will spark tremendous power and anointing to fulfill the Divine Will.

Leaders who spend little quality time being with the Lord end up building their kingdoms or something other than the Holy Temple of Christ. Rather than being builders and edifiers, they end up becoming demolition men, tearing down anything God is doing outside of their sphere. If a leader is not building the Temple of Christ, with Christ, for Christ, it is better to pause and examine motivations, and repent rather than to stand before the Presence of Almighty God to explain.

The substance of good leadership is edification—the building upward of the Temple of Christ. Such leaders will serve others gladly and will be willing to be served by others. Too many leaders are willing to serve other churches through preaching and teaching but are unwilling to receive others into their church, not trusting that God could minister to them through another servant or ministry. The building up of the Body has so far been with much struggle as the various organs dishonor and fight to tear down each other, causing sickness and diseases to form in the Body. Builders edify each other, building up the Temple in love for God to see it become *one Body*. These are the builders of the Last Day; friends of the Bridegroom whose concern is the preparation of the Bride.

However, as we work toward unity, it is important to be aware of the enemy's strategies. As the Holy Spirit works to bring the Body into union, there is also an ecumenical effort underway, promoted by the kingdom of darkness. This movement is seeking to unify churches and religions under the guise of good intentions and the banner of peace and love outside of the boundaries of the Word of God. This spirit seeks to confuse and distort the Heart of God for mankind.

The two spiritual forces of Heaven and Hell are both in the process of unification as the end times draw near. These two forces are separately at work fashioning and mobilizing the warriors that will comprise God's *Davidic Army* and the enemy's *Goliath'* in a face-off in the climax of the ages. Bringing everything under the rule of 'one' is the underlying motivation behind the New World Order, globalism, and the mega-mergers of corporations. Unification, as seen in mergers, acquisitions, NGOs, and the alliances of nations is working to hasten the day of the anti-Christ.

Presently, the Holy Spirit is actively establishing Divine connections within the Body so that it may stand as One Man. God's aim is not mere comradeship for the sake of unity; He is seeking a Holy union, tempered by His refining fire, thereby aligning the Body according to His ordained plan. This union, under His Lordship and direction, serves one purpose—to fulfill His Father's Will.

To think we possess the wisdom or understanding to connect *the parts* in constructing *the temple of the Christ* is presumption and imprudence. God alone holds the Blueprint and design of the Temple and the intricacy of how the parts fit together. Connections forged by the Holy Spirit will be robust, sparking immense Power.

The unification of the Body of Christ with its many divisions, denominations, and ministries is a mammoth undertaking. *The various parts must be willing to change procedure to come under the operation of the leadership of One*—the Lord Jesus Christ, having one vision—the summing up of all things in Christ. This is the stewardship leaders are called to, in this era. Only the Holy Spirit can pull this off and guarantee success. The Assembly of God cannot be a carnal enterprise comprised of many powerful agencies, each vying for power and attempting to retain control—it will be a crucified company of authentic apostolic leaders with all eyes fixed on Jesus.

Every leader chosen by God is led by Him to the place of surrender—where they willingly lose their lives to grant Him ultimate Power, control, wisdom, and Glory. God transcends carnal structures and does not take sides. He manifests His power to establish His 'new thing' on Earth outside of old paradigms. Leaders truly submitted to Him, with ears attuned to His guidance, will humbly shift to His side, embracing the form and model He has ordained to complete His work on Earth.

As we come together in obedience and humility God will make His will clear. He will release His plan and the strategies necessary to implement His plan. Divine networking will take place and strategic partnerships and alliances will then be forged. The Body will come together in one accord, with one mind, one vision, and one understanding to wait on God and the re-release of the Promise of the Father that will unite it as *One Awesome Man,* released into the earth for the conclusion of His Will.

Authentic apostolic\prophetic Scaffolding Produces Momentum:

The Apostolic/prophetic model of the last day will have traveled and completed the Journey to know and understand its every step. They have become so intimately acquainted with the path, that they quickly identify every stone of stumbling and every demonic trap. As guides, they are anointed to keep the pilgrims moving where they tend to stray into these traps. As guides, they fully understand the Blueprint of the Journey revealed in the Feasts of God, beginning with Passover and ending with the Feast of Tabernacles, which ushers in the establishment of the Throne of God on Earth.

The early apostles received and taught the full revelation of Christ—the whole counsel of God; but in later years, especially during the dark ages the pace of the journey steadily declined as the Light of God decreased with increased sin. However, over the centuries, true leaders, and guides with each passing generation, have gleaned deeper insights of the journey. Knowledge and understanding increased with each generation as precepts were built upon precepts. God will rein in all the parts to form a well-defined and efficient path that produces momentum and accelerates the movement of the children of God toward fullness in Christ.

Jesus builds His Temple in us individually and with us corporately. It is imperative to cease interfering with His work, as doing so will greatly expedite the process. Any interference or addition to the process, lacking His direction, only serves to hinder His work and oppose the objectives He seeks to achieve.

The Old Testament is characteristic of the law written on stone. The New is characteristic of Grace, through which the law is written on soft pliable hearts. In the Old Testament, they were commanded to obey or receive punishment. Grace in the New Testament gave God the flexibility to work in each heart at their own pace. Laws cannot, therefore, be rigid, as each person is at a different place of growth and only God can determine each one's needs and capacity at any given period. If we are to become one Body, it is important to get rid of the *fighting words*, lead by example, and infuse others with a hunger and a passion to press on to the Glory.

Defined methods and patterns hold greater significance in the early stages of development, especially for those adhering to worldly standards of goals, targets, and methods. While these elements play a crucial role in maintaining order in life, they do not represent the ultimate ideal which is *life in the Spirit and moving in harmony with Him to fulfill His purposes.* In this realm, we need not devise strategies and formulas—*He is it!* His directions are released precisely at the appointed time.

John the Baptist was the forerunner of Christ's first coming. He did not have methods, strategies, or target goals. He did not have any advertisements, a suit, or even a microphone, yet all Israel gathered unto him. All that John had was an anointing and a heart of obedience. The greatest lessons of leadership can all be summed up in just two verses of Scripture:

"You shall love the Lord your God with all your heart, with all your soul, and with all your strength." Deuteronomy 6:5

"Trust in the Lord with all your heart and lean not on your understanding; in all your ways acknowledge Him, and He will direct your paths." Proverbs 3:5

Nathan the prophet told David that his plan to build God a house was a good one and that he should go ahead. However, God had another plan. We work with the Lord to build His Temple only as He allows us to participate—He is the builder, and He has the plan. As we align ourselves with Him, the entire process accelerates, gaining momentum as dispersed energy from presumptive activities is consolidated and directed toward a specific path and target.

This concentration and direction of the Body's energy resembles harnessing and converting energy into power, similar to the redirecting of the force of Niagara Falls. The accumulated insights, understanding, and wisdom over centuries form a potent and efficient energy source—a compounded reservoir of divine insight and revelation. By skillfully directing this flow, energy is not only created but also harnessed, producing increased power and efficiency, and ultimately reducing the time to complete the race. This generation of emerging warriors stands poised to reap the benefits of this extraordinary phenomenon.

The pace of the journey is now about to accelerate and build momentum. We are about to receive a Holy Ghost Power surge that will propel us into the next *kairos* season of God's time. The cities of the nations of the world will not be impacted by the Power of God until the leaders who sit at the gates begin to work together on behalf of the people of the city. Jeremiah prophesied that the adversary would establish his throne at the city gates. Only through the collaborative efforts of leaders can this intrusion be prevented.

Just as God has been building the Temple of the Christ over the centuries, Satan has been busy at work building his beast of which he is the head. David and Goliath are soon about to clash in the war of the ages. Are we like David, Joshua, or Caleb, ready to take on the giants? Jesus is coming back to walk this Earth once again in the prepared Body of David's Tabernacle.

We will be witnesses to great signs and wonders as the early church, and as Moses and Israel witnessed, as God moves to set a great harvest of souls free from bondage to Pharaoh. The Earth will experience the greatest prison break of all history since Moses led the people of Israel out of Egypt. As He did in the time of Moses, God has heard the cries, and He is coming down in Power to deliver His people. When He comes, judgment will be released upon spiritual Babylon as His mighty arm comes down in wrath upon the kingdom of Satan's world system. This judgment will extend to every facet that upholds or sustains this system.

The union that comes from those who unite in obedience—Israel and the Gentile church, male and female, young and old, rich, and poor, prophets and apostles, evangelists, and teachers—all aligned with the mind of Christ, will give birth to His Glorious Bride. The holy anointing oil cascading from the Head of this Temple, streaming over the Body, conforms it to the order, submission, and obedience inherent in true apostolic leadership united with Christ.

The Bride of Christ embedded in the very Life of Christ will possess His strength to overcome the enemy in the Power and Might of Yahweh.

"Oh, the depths of the riches both of the wisdom and knowledge of God, how unsearchable are His judgments, and His ways past finding out! For who has known the mind of the Lord? Or who has become His counselor? Or who has first given to Him and it shall be repaid to Him? For of Him and through Him and to Him are all things, to whom be glory forever. Amen." Romans 11:33-3

Chapter Eighteen

WHAT ARE YOU BUILDING?

"But each one should build with care. For no one can lay any foundation other than the one already laid, which is Jesus Christ. If anyone builds on this foundation using gold, silver, costly stones, wood, hay or straw, their work will be shown for what it is, because the Day will bring it to light. It will be revealed with fire, and the fire will test the quality of each person's work." 1 Corinthians 3:10-13

W hen empowered by the Holy Spirit, we gain the ability to lead lives of holiness pleasing to God. The Holy Spirit becomes our supreme authority. What He says goes. He works through the Word, revealing it to the hungry soul, and never goes against it. He intricately shapes and molds the diverse organs within the Body of Christ, each possessing a distinct uniqueness, yet collectively crafted to mirror, *"in part"* the image of Christ.

> *"For we know in part and we prophesy in part. But when that which is perfect has come, then that which is in part will be done away." 1 Corinthians 13:9*

The Greek word for 'in part' is *meros* and means; *to get as a section; a division or a share; a portion.* The word for *'perfect'* is *teleios,* meaning *complete in labor, growth, and character, of full age, perfect.* We can, therefore, conclude from this Scripture that no one has the whole revelation. Each has been designated a share to steward and a specific function to contribute to the grand culmination of the majestic realization of *the Christ.*

At the time when union in the Body is realized, in the time to *"awaken love,"* wherein all components converge into a sacred, holy offering to God, the *"perfect"* will be unveiled—*man in union with God* (Songs 8:4). The finished structure then emerges, the matured individual and corporate body, fully developed in stature, work, and character, filled with the fullness of deity.

It is possible, on the Journey of the ascent to Christ, to be moving in the Spirit, yet regarding a certain doctrine, remain fixed and stagnant, failing to advance in knowledge and comprehension. This static state can lead to becoming confined by particular aspects of these truths, essentially becoming imprisoned by them. The Holy Spirit, however, persists in moving forward, bestowing greater revelation, and understanding to those who are open to hearing, receiving, and continuing on the Journey.

It is possible to be a part of a very dynamic church or ministry, empowered by the Holy Spirit and bearing fruit, yet on certain issues the leadership and the saints are not growing. If this is left unchecked, this can act as leaven, having the ability to leaven the whole lump. Such churches or ministries can be unaware that they are in a box. Their ministries or churches may appear very spacious and beautiful, the boundaries of which can hardly be seen, yet the walls are there, nonetheless.

Once we anchor ourselves to a *fixed position* (beyond the fundamental principles), the risk of being confined or imprisoned by it becomes a reality. The Body of Christ is on a forward movement toward growth, expanding in wisdom, knowledge, and power in proportion to its humility, as it makes its way toward the Light and the fullness of Christ. It must be open to allow the Spirit to break down old mindsets and ways of seeing things and allow Him to demolish our prison walls.

This dispensation is passing through or transitioning as He works to position us in His Will, Mind, and Word toward the fulfillment and conclusion of His purposes in Christ. God is shattering old ways that have become irrelevant while introducing new ways for the challenges of the hour to achieve His purposes and align them with a fresh revelation of His intent through His Word. He is trimming away the excesses, cutting out dead procedure, firing unproductive managers, and bringing in a whole new crew of workers, young and old, male, and female of every nation and tribe, from many streams, who have ears to hear and are willing to obey and work with Him.

This is precisely what took place in the Book of Acts. God brought in a whole new crew and smashed every aspect of lifeless religion. He gathered a raggedy army of men who chose to give Him first place and transformed them into a powerful force to be reckoned with. Jesus is the owner and C.E.O of the Body. He must have freedom and full access—no restrictions, no boundaries to restrain Him other than the law of the Spirit of Life under His administration.

In the days to come, leaders of churches and individual believers will find themselves in the valley of decision. The choice will be whether to hold to the Truth and make their stand on the Word of God or to embrace the liberal views of the world in their lives and their churches. This is an especially important time for the leadership of churches; some will face the very difficult decision to break away from mainstream denominational churches and seeker-friendly churches that are going the way of Balaam, selling their souls to the gods of this world that entice the children of God to fall into gross sin.

The gods of this world are presently moving in, to set up thrones and altars in many of the traditional Protestant churches and the Catholic church. God's heart is for the people plagued by these spirits; He died for all, *"while we were yet sinners."* Even so, leaders in the Body of Christ cannot embrace these gods as they work in opposition to God's Word, all that God is, and all that He is building. They work to undermine His transcendent purposes for the coming forth of His Bride in purity and righteousness.

The Human Immunodeficiency Virus—HIV, wreaks havoc on the immune system—the body's defense mechanism, often as a result of sexual behavior God calls sin. In the spirit, it strips away God's favor, power, and anointing—*the spiritual defense system of the Body of Christ,* leaving it vulnerable to spiritual assaults. God considers sin a deviation from His design and craftsmanship in humanity. Consequently, as a measure to safeguard spiritual integrity, it becomes necessary to be distanced from those who advocate the acceptability and embrace of sin among leaders.

The ongoing spiritual battle is ferocious, and the Body has become increasingly susceptible to attacks causing some leaders to align themselves with the forces of darkness. The pervasive influence of the anti-Christ spirit seeks to sow discord within numerous denominations, leading many churches to separate themselves from affiliations that condone sinful practices. Nevertheless, it is crucial to remember that God possesses the remarkable ability to transform the malevolent intentions of Satan into opportunities for good, according to His Divine purposes. When division works to divide *soul from spirit,* it can be a good thing as Paul stated:

> *"For there must also be factions among you, that those who are approved may be recognised among you." 1 Corinthians 11:18*

The radiant brilliance of God's Light will illuminate the earth when the Body is transformed into the image of Christ. Those who have been deceived will be allowed to behold His Light and turn toward the Truth. True believers steadfastly stand on the side of righteousness, without compromise, regardless of the associated costs. It is through this unwavering commitment that the power to save lives and effect change is gained.

God requires a unified body of leaders, changed in the refining fires of *conformity to His image,* to stand aligned with Him in His purposes. Through such an alignment the Divine destiny God intends for Earth can be realized.

God is presently shaking His Body and chipping away at all that does not measure up to the Standard of His Son, or line up with His Plumb Line of His life. He is exposing blatant rebellious sin, first in His leaders, to remove all that has no part in Him. Churches and people who choose to remain under the covering of leaders rebelliously involved in open and gross sin that God calls an abomination are bringing themselves under the curses of God and opening themselves to evil spirits (Lev.18:22).

"I call heaven and earth as witness today against you, that I have set before you life and death, blessing and cursing; therefore choose life..." Deuteronomy 30:19

The Lord is hindered from moving to fulfill His purposes through a twenty-first-century Pharisaic church, locked in a prison of its dogmatic opinions, founded upon secular views and not on the Word of God. As His people, we must remain vigilant and discern His movements, forsaking the dead weight of sin and rigid religious mindsets.

God is now gathering an army of end-time leaders who will work with Him to build Him a *Most Holy Place*. As the Word says, *"Holy, Holy, Holy is the LORD God Almighty,"* the whole earth will be full of His Glory. A New Wineskin is emerging, a new structure, distinct from the ones that have served His purposes in the past. This structure has only *One LORD* and will be built upon the teamwork of a unified leadership.

As an army of apostles, prophets, evangelists, and teachers collaborate harmoniously, the Holy Spirit is poised to reinstate Divine order within the Church. Together, they embark on constructing a Temple that authentically mirrors Christ, carefully aligned to His Word. Rather than relying on rigid rules, regulations, and laws, this army undertakes its mission by exemplifying the profound humility and submission to the Father embodied in Christ.

These leaders will stand out in their roles as spiritual fathers and mothers, embodying the wisdom, humility, and submission that are characterized by Christ. From this emerging Wineskin, Godly submission to Spirit-led direction will come forth within the Church.

ESSENTIAL PREREQUISITES OF LEADERSHIP

Two essential prerequisites stand out for an apostle or church leader, both of which are crucial. The primary requirement is that they must have encountered Christ or be actively progressing on their journey toward a meeting with Him.

> *"Am I not an apostle? Am I not free? Have I not seen Jesus Christ our Lord? Are you not my work in the Lord?"* *1Corinthians 9:1*

The original apostles were not only acquainted with Jesus but also bore witness to His resurrection (Acts 1:22). Encounters with Christ don't necessarily have to mirror the extraordinary experiences of Paul or the disciples. What *is crucial* is that those entrusted with leadership, responsible for building the House of the Lord, have devoted substantial time at His feet, immersed in His Divine Presence.

Builders of the Temple must have made the climb to the pinnacle of the mountain to behold Christ. Each builder and leader have a designated Divine appointment with God to receive the blueprint for their specific portion of the Temple. Such sacred encounters serve as the foundation for building and leading in alignment with the Divine plan. *How can one build what one has not first seen?* If we haven't seen Christ who is the Pattern, then what is being built?

The second imperative is that builders and apostles, those commissioned and sent by God, must comprehend the overarching Blueprint. They collaborate with other builders, extending their efforts beyond local boundaries to build translocally. Possessing a global revelation of the Divine Majesty of the Body of Christ, they actively engage with other leaders in the work. These authentic apostolic leaders—*friends of the Bridegroom*, will love, honor, and be willing to serve the Bride, not just their portion.

Every builder must embark on a solitary journey to the mountaintop, entering the Holy of Holies to receive revelation. Relying on second-hand information can be inadequate unless the revelation of others is fully apprehended and received in the spirit. The risk of straying from the authentic pattern and foundational principles of Christ will result in a structure similar to the leaning Tower of Pisa, *in constant need of being propped up*. With second-hand revelations, leaders can be left vulnerable to deception, and susceptible to manipulation or persuasion that could undermine commitment to the work.

Leaders who have not been to the top of the mountain to receive revelation, in times of storms and great testing will be easily persuaded to capitulate and surrender their position. Those who have *seen* will persevere with the vision, will have power with God, and will stay the course with apostolic resolution.

THE ABSENCE OF LAWS

Regulations and laws are deliberately vague in the New Testament for three particularly important reasons. The first is that the Body is being conformed to the measurement of Christ—*a person*, not to a set of rules. We are being built up *into His Life*, to look, walk, and think *like Him*, a process established on relationship. We are being conformed to Him through the submission of our wills in this process. He is the Pattern. It has little to do with titles and semantics, and everything to do with obedience, submission, humility, love, and intimate relationships.

The second reason is that we are now led by the Holy Spirit, not by adherence to law. Nevertheless, the Holy Spirit operates within the realms of order, submission, and the Word of God, uniquely molding and placing each life in the grand design of the

Body of Christ. Unconfined by rigid regulations, the Holy Spirit provides the necessary structure for each organ in the Body to fulfill its purpose and function harmoniously—all within the broad parameters prescribed for church governance.

A third rationale for the New Testament's ambiguity regarding structure is rooted in humanity's inclination to default to rigid rules and methodologies, resulting in the undesirable fruit of self-righteousness. Inevitably, inflexible patterns, rules, and regulations condemn us to a church life dominated by works-based self-righteousness. Such frameworks dethrone Christ and undermine the Lordship of the Holy Spirit in the ongoing construction of His House.

When God blesses, most will immediately conclude that they are favored and have the right pattern. It is then easy to fall into self-righteousness and pride. This echoes the attitude of the Pharisee who, in prayer, proclaimed, *"I am grateful I am not like them."* Too many believe they are the chosen ones on the cutting edge of God's work. This mindset has to be discarded for the *One New Man* Christ died for, to emerge, tasked with constructing the concluding phase of the Temple—the Most Holy Place of Christ.

God's work manifests uniquely in individuals, churches, ministries, and nations, each bearing its distinct insight, revelation, flavor, appearance, and timing. Despite this diversity, there exists a common belief among some that there is a singular rule that should be universally applied to all. This tendency, however, risks dismissing anything beyond one's current understanding, as not of God's doing.

The moment there is an insistence based on dogmatic religious belief, for example, that women cannot be leaders in governmental offices, or divorced people cannot be elders or hold an office, we inadvertently create laws, and a box for ourselves in which God is restricted and imprisoned. These rigid laws shut off the flow of the Power of the work of the Cross that transforms men and women who have been divorced, alcoholics, homosexuals, adulterers, and even murderers into great and mighty leaders in the kingdom of God—*as He did in the Bible.*

The Holy Spirit is God, and He is free to work as He sees fit. Religion and legalism can hide in *any pattern.* Patterns, models, and methods belong in the Holy Place, which was meant to act only as a scaffold into the Holy of Holies where nothing of flesh can live. Should any pattern begin to assume the Holy Spirit's role as Lord in directing the Body, the focus has shifted from the Lord to the pattern—which has then become an idol.

The moment a pattern becomes set in stone, or a wineskin becomes inflexible in its methods, it is in danger of becoming a lifeless religion. The Wineskin of the end times will be very flexible, and fluid—having the nature to be shaped into an organ that serves the purposes of the Holy Spirit. The Wineskin of 'The Bride' of the end times cannot be static, passive, or stationary; it will change form as it undergoes its metamorphosis into 'The Christ.' Anything not moving is a target and becomes stagnant and foul. The opposite of static is dynamic, meaning *active; potent; a force in operation.*

The word dynamic is from the root word *dunamis* meaning *power.* The Wineskin of the Body of Christ in the time of the conclusion of the ages, will have been transformed into one that is fluid and characterized by Life and Power. It will have the ability, nature, and dynamic to contain the New Wine and *dunamis* Power of God.

SECTION IV

PREPARE THE WAY

"Prepare the way of the LORD; Make straight in the desert

A highway for our God. Every valley shall be exalted

And every mountain and hill brought low;

The crooked places shall be made straight

And the rough places smooth;

The glory of the LORD shall be revealed,

And all flesh shall see *it* together;

For the mouth of the LORD has spoken."

Isaiah 40:3-5

Chapter Nineteen

THE MESSENGER

"The City is laid out as a square; its length is as great as its breadth. And he measured the city with the reed: twelve thousand furlongs. Its length, breadth, and height are equal." Revelation 21:16

Over the years I have sought the Lord for the significance of the number twelve and multiples of twelve: twenty-four to one hundred and forty-four thousand. Why twelve? To understand, let's delve into some heavenly mathematics and numbers significant to God. In every aspect of the structure of the Heavenly Jerusalem—God's New Creation, and Temple, the Trinity is prevalent. God, as the Architect of this City, designed it as a perfect cube having four sides. The number four is representative of the *New Creation* hence *four hundred years* before Israel was released from Egypt to inherit the Promised Land, and *four thousand years* from Abraham to the completion of the Temple at the end of the age and the beginning of the Kingdom reign of Christ. The book of Revelation references the four corners of the Earth (Rev. 7:1, 20:8).

On each of the four sides of the Great City, there are *three gates* leading into the City—three representing *the Trinity of the Godhead.* In Heavenly Mathematics, the Trinity times the New Creation—represented by four, gives a total of *twelve gates.* Using the same principle, the Trinity plus the New Creation gives us *seven*, the number of completion and perfection.

The approximate *four thousand years* from the time Abraham left Ur to the present season, is the approximate boundary and square area of time allotted for the construction and completion of God's New Creation. This is the time for God's *New Man* to grow up and be completed to the stature of the Fullness of Christ.

This *construction area of time* to build the City is also pictured prophetically in Israel's deliverance from bondage to Pharaoh after 400 years. After that time, they were released to possess the Land Promised by God. That *four-hundred-year span*, as is the *four-thousand-year span*, reaching into the present, reflects the time also allocated for evil to rise to its fullness. At the appointed time, it will then be purged by the Mighty hand of God. In God's wisdom, time has been given for the evil *tares* to grow just as *the iniquity of the Amorites grows to its fullness* (Matt. 13, Gen. 15:16).

ON HUNDRED & FORTY-FOUR

"Then he measured its wall: one hundred and forty-four cubits, according to the measure of a man, that is, of an angel." Revelation 21:17

This passage was also a great puzzle to me. I know that some have interpreted this passage to mean that the angel used the human measurement of cubits. However, the Greek word for *angel* in this passage is *aggelos* which also means *messenger*. It is the same word used in the *seven letters* sent to the *angels of the churches* in the Book of Revelation and is commonly thought to represent the *leadership of those churches*. I believe rather that the height of the wall of the Heavenly City is a Heavenly measurement representing *the Messenger—Christ in union with man—an army of apostolic leaders!*

"Behold, I will send My messenger, and He will prepare the way before Me. And the Lord whom you seek, will suddenly come to His temple, even the Messenger of the covenant…" Malachi 3:1

The City of God—the Heavenly Jerusalem is the measure of the fullness of Christ. A majestic City radiating His light and Glory. It has no need of light as He is *its Light;* it has no need of a temple as He is *its Temple.* Every detail and measurement of this structure represents Christ—the length, breadth, width, and height. The City is a testament to His transcendent work to draw the *sons of God* into a Holy union within Himself—*His finished work.* It is the unveiling of His Masterpiece—a Divine and sublime structure surpassing natural thought and reasoning.

ONE HUNDRED & FORTY-FOUR THOUSAND

The number twelve and multiples of twelve throughout Scripture are also representative of the *completed Israel of God*—the twelve tribes including the Gentile saints grafted into Judah. It also represents Divine leadership and governance of the Body expressed through *the twelve Jewish apostles in union with Christ.* Leadership in Biblical times was given authority to guard and govern the City at the *twelve gates* that gave entrance into this City. Each Gate was given the name of one of the *twelve tribes* of Israel. The implication is that each tribe in the Body was given the authority and responsibility to guard and man the Gates of the City of God.

God's governmental leadership are the firstfruits of *Christ,* conformed to His image. In Revelations chapter seven, the angels are told to withhold judgment on the earth until the *servants of God* are all sealed on the forehead. O*ne hundred and forty-four thousand are sealed*—twelve thousand from each tribe, representing the government and *Commonwealth of the Israel of God*—a picture of the completeness of *the Temple of the Christ.*

> *"Do not harm the earth, the sea, or the trees till we have sealed the servants of our God on their foreheads." Revelation 7:3*

> *"They were purchased from among men and offered as firstfruits to God and to the Lamb." Revelation 14:4*

These 144,000 servants represent the apostolic leadership of the *One New Man* of Jewish and Gentile leaders in a Divine union. Gentile saints have been grafted into the *Lion of the tribe of Judah* and now comprise a key component of *the Israel of God* (Rom. 11:24-26). Together with Christ, they become a Body of apostolic/prophetic leadership He inhabits to fulfill the Father's will and His purposes on Earth.

APOSTOLIC/PROPHETIC MESSENGERS

During the season of trials and tribulation, before Christ's Return in Glory, He will return in Power to this Body, through whom He will demonstrate His manifold wisdom to principalities and powers. The apostolic/prophetic is a Body prepared for Him to complete His work. Together they work to prepare the way for His Return in Glory.

> *"...but a body You have prepared for Me. ...Then I said, 'Behold I have come ... To do Your will, O God.'" Hebrews 10:5-7*

This Body has been undergoing a metamorphosis, or evolution of growth with each successive generation over history. Each era has given rise to a new crop of leaders imbued with fresh vision and revelations. Over history, every generation has yielded exceptional leaders who, as beacons of light, courageously stood against the tide of wickedness and resistance to God's will.

As apostolic leadership builds to prepare *a place for* the Lord, the prophetic is the trumpet that prepares the *way for* His Return. These two anointings work together to both pronounce and announce the Lord's intentions. The prophetic functions to keep the work moving and directed toward Christ as the apostle builds. The ministry of the prophets will be essential in keeping the Body focused on Christ, through stressful and highly charged times in the season before He returns.

The Return of Christ is the most Glorious, awesome, and wonderful event of all History and all eternity; however, the labor pains the Earth will endure to bring forth this great event will be *hard labor* of a magnitude equally as great:

> *"For then there will be great tribulation, such as has not been since the beginning of the world until this time, no, nor ever shall be" Matthew 24:21*

In times of *impending judgment,* God will send *prophet messengers* such as Jeremiah, Isaiah, and Ezekiel, to herald messages to warn, and call for a return to God through repentance. In the times of *deliverance from a time of judgment,* God will send *prophet deliverers* such as Deborah and Daniel, to announce the time of deliverance. God will arm His people with the strategies necessary for battle and for the period after deliverance. Both types are *prophet messengers* yet carry different messages for different times and seasons.

The generation that *prepares the way for the Lord's second coming,* will give birth to an unprecedented corporate body of exceptional leadership, *marked* as radical bondslaves to Christ. They emerge from the Fire as *One Man,* moving with one mind and having one heart. They are the fruit of God's work born from the process of death and resurrection. These leaders are friends of the Bridegroom who work with Christ to bring forth the Bride in Glory, backed by a powerful anointing from Heaven.

These leaders will fulfill and complete God's purposes, to prepare and build with the sword in hand, as they bring the harvest safely into this House. They will march out in power against the enemy to defeat evil, guard the gates, and defend the City of God. They will perform the *greater things of God* and enter a scale of the dimension of the miraculous not previously known.

The *One New Man* that is the Headstone, comes forth in the maturity of times. These servants are called and chosen for the hour. Together they are sealed with the name of God on their foreheads—*Yahweh Shamah, the Lord is there! (Ez. 48:35).*

"Then I looked, and behold, a Lamb standing on Mount Zion, and with Him one hundred and forty-four thousand, having His Father's name written on their foreheads." Revelation 14:1

Many say that Christ could return at any moment, but Jesus cannot return until obedience is complete (2 Cor. 10:5-6), the times of the restoration of all things have begun (Acts 3:21), the *sons of God* are revealed (Rom. 8:18-22), and a measure of Israel is restored to her place as the head and not the tail, receives Christ and declares, *"Blessed is He who comes in the name of the Lord"* (Matt. 23:39).

These *sons of God* who have completed their obedience are the leaders chosen for this hour. They will not satisfy themselves with partial obedience like Saul or even Moses but will walk like Jesus, *"obedient unto death."* (Phil.2:8). They will be the midwives of this historic time on earth, through whom God will bring forth the King and His Kingdom. These obedient soldiers from Israel and the nations of the world are the Messengers who work together with the Lord to begin the process of restoring all things in the season of Jesus' Return. The closer we come to the end-times the closer we come to the union of Christ's Body of *Jew and Gentile, male and female, and slave and free.* We are moving forward toward unification.

The seven letters to the churches mentioned in Revelations chapters two and three are words of warning to the corporate Body of Christ. The admonitions in these letters find relevance and are applicable wherever they resonate. The seven blessings in these letters are given to those who overcome and endure to the end. God will *keep—not take out—*the faithful through the hour of trial to come upon the Earth (Rev. 3:10). The Greek word for the phrase *keep you from,* is *tereo* and can also mean *keep you through* (used in 2 Cor.13:4).

As the world approaches the conclusion of the ages, the closer we are to the Father's answer to Jesus' prayer that His leaders would be *one* and that His Body would become *one* through their unity. Jesus' prayer for His apostles who began His work is also His prayer for the apostolic leadership he has chosen to *complete his work*.

> "*I pray for them. I do not pray for the world but for those whom you have given Me, for they are Yours. And all mine are Yours, and Yours are Mine, and I am glorified in them. Now I am no longer in the world, and I come to You. Holy Father, keep through Your name those whom you have given Me, that they may be one as We are...* **I do not pray that You should take them out of the world, but that You should keep them from the evil one.** *They are not of the world, just as I am not of the world. Sanctify them by Your truth. Your word is truth. As you sent Me into the world, I also have sent them into the world...*
>
> *I do not pray for these alone, but also for those who will believe in Me through their word; that they all may be one, as You, Father, are in Me, and I in You; that they also may be one in Us, that the world may believe that You sent Me. And the glory which you gave Me I have given them,* **that they may be one just as We are one:** *I in Them, and You in Me; that they may be made perfect in one, and that the world may know that You have sent Me, and have loved them as You have loved Me.*" John 17:9-23 (emphasis mine)

The leaders being prepared for this hour will be the hands and feet through whom Christ will walk in this time to heal the sick, raise the dead, and perform signs and wonders. During this time these leaders who carry Christ's burden for the harvest will stand as strong towers to strengthen the weak hands and the feeble knees, to remind and encourage those who are fearful, that God is coming to save.

> "*Strengthen the weak hands and make firm the feeble and tottering knees. Say to those who are of a fearful and hasty heart, Be strong, fear not! Behold, your God will come with*

vengeance; with the recompense of God He will come and save you. Then the eyes of the blind shall be opened, and the ears of the deaf shall be unstopped" Isaiah 35:3 AMPC

The occurrence of the rapture will coincide with the resounding blast of the last trumpet, preceding the outpouring of the bowls of God's wrath (1 Cor. 15:52). Revelation chapter 14 shows the 144,000 in Heaven at the time of *the reaping of the Earth.* A heavenly scene unfolds showing one like the Son of Man on clouds with angels reaping two harvests of the earth—the wheat and the tares (Matt. 13). The wheat is reaped by the one who is *like the Son of Man*, and the tares are reaped by the angel with a sharp sickle and another who had power over Fire—they are thrown into the winepress of the wrath of God.

The leadership of God's House stands with Him until their purpose on Earth is fulfilled.

"A man will be a hiding place from the wind, and a cover from the tempest, as rivers of water in a dry place, as the shadow of a great rock in a weary land." Isaiah 32:2

Chapter Twenty

BENJAMIN LEADS

"They have seen Your procession, O God, The procession of my God, my King, into the sanctuary. The singers went before, the players on instruments followed after; Among them were the maidens playing timbrels. Bless God in the congregations, The Lord, from the fountain of Israel. There is little Benjamin, their leader..." Psalm 68:24-27

The leaders chosen to prepare the way of the Lord are being formed as a tribe in the likeness of the tribe of Benjamin. Benjamin held a significant place in the heart of God and his father Jacob. The City of Jerusalem was positioned in the Land allotted to Benjamin, that bordered Judah. These two tribes became a coalition after the other ten tribes chose to align with Jeroboam instead of Rehoboam 1Kgs. 12:21).

Jesus entered the arena of mankind through the tribe of Judah at His first coming; He will return to Jerusalem, the place of His Throne, through a tribe of Leaders fashioned in the likeness of Benjamin. Benjamin was a warrior-like tribe noted for their boldness, ferocious courage, and their savage violence toward the enemy. They were known for *using both the right hand and the left in hurling stones and shooting arrows with the bow* (1Chr. 12:2). Benjamin is a warrior tribe representing the new breed arising for the hour. When blessing each of his sons, Jacob said of Benjamin:

"Benjamin is a ravenous wolf; in the morning he shall devour the prey, and at night he shall divide the spoil." Genesis 49:27

Benjamin represents the Headstone made of *adamant stone*. They are the sons who will break forth from the womb of the morning on the third day, in the Day of His power (Ps. 110:3). The blessing declared over Benjamin by Moses prophesies of God's sovereign protection and covering over him. God guards him and *keeps* him as he dwells between His shoulders.

> *"Let the beloved of the Lord rest secure in him, for he shields him all day long, and the one the LORD loves rests between his shoulders." Deuteronomy33:12 NIV*

The tribe fashioned in the vein of Benjamin will lead the battle in the last days having been trained in fire to withstand great persecution. Psalm 91 is written for the Benjamin tribe of whom a thousand will fall at their side and ten thousand at their right hand, but it will not come near him. This tribe of Benjamin leaders is represented in the 144,000 servants who will rise to the measure of the completed Man of the stature of Christ. They will sit as God's appointed and anointed government at the Gates of the City of God guarding His investment.

BENJAMIN IS BIRTHED THROUGH STRUGGLE

As was discussed in earlier chapters, the length, breadth, and height of the City of Jerusalem are designed as equal, each being twelve thousand furlongs (Rev. 21:16). The word translated furlong, is the Greek word *stadion* which means; *a certain measure of distance; by implication a stadium or racecourse—race.* We can understand from this that the length, breadth, and height of the City not only give us the *size* of the structure but also a *perception of the race* toward its completion. It is the same word Paul uses to describe his race.

> *"I've done all this so that I would become God's partner for the sake of the gospel. Isn't it obvious that all runners on the racetrack keep on running to win, but only one receives the victor's prize? Yet each one of you must run the race to be victorious. A true athlete will be disciplined in every respect,*

practicing constant self-control in order to win a laurel wreath that quickly withers. But we run our race to win a victor's crown that will last forever. For that reason, I don't run just for exercise or box like one throwing aimless punches, but I train like a champion athlete. I subdue my body and get it under my control, so that after preaching the good news to others I myself won't be disqualified" 1 Corinthians 9:23-27 TPT

The City of Jerusalem rises as a monument to victory in the love struggle of obedience. Like Christ, these sons of obedience have been anointed for burial in *myrrh,* which means bitter. Like Esther, they have been prepared in the oil of myrrh to walk with conviction in the way of, *"If I perish, I perish."* Like Mary, whose name means bitter or myrrh, a sword has pierced their souls (Lk. 2:35), Like Eve, *"...in pain, you shall bring forth..."* and Rachel, *"Benjamin"—Son of my strength and my right arm"* (Gen 3:16).

"Then they journeyed from Bethel. And when there was but a little distance to go to Ephrath, Rachel labored in childbirth, and she had hard labor. Now it came to pass, when she was in hard labor, that the midwife said to her, "Do not fear; you will have this son also." And so it was, as her soul was departing (for she died), that she called his name Ben-Oni; but his father called him Benjamin." Genesis 35:16-18

The things that God sometimes gives us to eat may be bitter to our taste but in time they will become sweet if we persevere with Him. He will take our *"Ben-oni"—son of our sorrow* and turn it into *"Ben-jamin"—Son of His Right Arm, son of His strength.* Sorrow may last for the night, but joy will come in the morning when the Morning Star rises to take His place on the Throne.

The measurement of the wall of the City was 144,000 cubits— both the wall and the number represent governance and leadership. The character of the *Messenger of God* comprised of the 144,000 from all tribes, forged in the likeness of Benjamin, comes forth through *hard labor* and great struggle. The cost of their preparation is measured in the sorrow, bitterness, pain, and struggle to come forth into the fullness of Christ. As He did with Paul, God reveals His Son through these sons, in their struggle to persevere—this is the *hard labor* to birth Benjamin—*son of My strength.*

> *"But when it pleased God, who separated me from my mother's womb and called* me *through His grace, to reveal His Son in me, that I might preach Him among the Gentiles, I did not immediately confer with flesh and blood..." Galatians 1:16*

PURCHASING PROPERTY IN BENJAMIN

Before God's judgment was released on Israel through Babylon and their captivity began, God instructed Jeremiah to go and buy property in the land of Benjamin. According to the law and custom of that time, one deed of purchase was to be sealed and one to remain open. Jeremiah instructed that both deeds were to be placed in a clay jar to last for a long time. This prophetic act was given as a revelation that Israel would one day return to the Promised Land (Jer. 32).

> *"Thus says the LORD of hosts, the God of Israel: "Take these deeds, both this purchase deed which is sealed and this deed which is open, and put them in an earthen vessel, that they may last many days." For thus says the LORD of hosts, the God of Israel: "Houses and fields and vineyards shall be possessed again in this land." Jeremiah 32:14*

The prophecy of the *open deed* was fulfilled under Cyrus when the people of Israel were released to return to rebuild the City of Jerusalem. The *sealed deed* represented the Messiah and was partially fulfilled by His first coming to Jerusalem, His crucifixion, and burial in the earthen vessel of human flesh. Jeremiah paid seventeen shekels, valued at approximately 30 pieces of silver—the price paid to Judas to betray Jesus. Jesus' burial and resurrection— the *breaking open of the sealed Promise* was the guarantee that after a second dispersion, the people of Israel would return a second time, and with the Lord's Return would be gathered to the Land forever.

> *"Then what was spoken by Jeremiah the prophet was fulfilled: "They took the thirty pieces of silver, the price set on him by the people of Israel, and they used them to buy the potter's field, as the Lord commanded me." Matthew 27:9*

God is now establishing a breed of leadership from all tribes, committed to investing in the Land, in the legacy of Benjamin, by their embrace of Israel. The Lord's work in these Benjamite leaders is His *deed of purchase* placed in these vessels of clay, sealed with *His Name*. After crossing through a time of darkness, a time of birthing in *hard labor*, Jesus, the *Son of God's Right Hand* will rise in the *sons of God* to reclaim the Promised Land from where He will rule and reign.

THE UNBROKEN NET OF UNITY

In John chapter twenty-one, Jesus acted out a prophetic parable of the last days. Peter, after a traumatic period of preparation in the fire, before, during, and after the Cross, in despair decided he was going back to fishing. Jesus was nowhere to be found and Peter reasoned that he was not wasting time waiting. The others decided to follow suit. They spend a long-wasted night in frustration, as they catch nothing.

In the morning Jesus showed up on the shore. He then asked them, possibly with gentle sarcasm, if they had caught any fish, to which they answered *no*. He tells them to throw their nets on the right side and they will find fish. The catch is so large they cannot draw it in. They caught one hundred and fifty-three fish and the net was unbroken.

John, the one closest to the heart of the Lord, recognized that it was Jesus and told Peter who immediately put on his outer garment to meet the Lord. Peter dove into the sea as the others followed in the boat with the fish. They were about two hundred cubits or measures from Jesus. He was on the shore waiting with the meal He had prepared for them.

The seven disciples in the boat represent the *'Israel of God'*—the saints amid the Great Sea of humanity. The one hundred and fifty-three large fish represent the people of the nations of the world. The fact that the fish is large means that there will be a large catch from every tribe.

Peter, who was the apostle sent to the Jews, stands as a representation of Israel. He puts back on his outer garment to meet Jesus, showing that Israel will put on her garment of salvation and robes of righteousness to meet her Messiah. As Peter takes the lead, so will Israel take the lead in this tribe of Benjamite leaders. These seven disciples represent the whole House of God, bringing in the whole catch, but Peter representing Israel hands them to the Lord, a beautiful picture of unity between the Gentile body of believers and Israel, and completion of God's work in Israel.

The *unbroken net* represents the unity required between all apostolic networks of the Body to bring in this Great Harvest at the end of the age. The net thrown over the right side represents *the Son* in union with the company of Benjamite leaders, positioned at the right hand of God. These *sons of God's Right Arm* will choose the way of unity to bring in God's Harvest, for the sake of Jesus and the Kingdom of God.

After a long night showing little fruit, the Body is about to bring forth a tribe who will get it right by their obedience to do things God's way. God is now preparing this tribe of leaders to lead the Body through the gauntlet of the last days. As Jesus was, so will they be persecuted by the religious Pharisees of this day.

"Woe to you, scribes and Pharisees, hypocrites! For you are like whitewashed tombs which indeed appear beautiful outwardly, but inside are full of dead men's bones and all uncleanness. Even

so you also outwardly appear righteous to men, but inside you are full of hypocrisy and lawlessness." Matthew 23:27-28

Jesus ended this chapter by marking these religious leaders as those who *kill the prophets sent by the Lord.* Jesus then begins Matthew twenty-four with the prophetic word that the entire temple of legalism, religion, and hypocrisy would be brought down. This is a word for today. Jesus is about to bring down all that has been built through carnal strength and agendas, Pharisee-ism, legalism, and religion. God is about to rise and judge this temple:

When the disciples asked Him when this would take place, He went into a lengthy discourse on the period many refer to as the *Great Tribulation.* The Body of Christ will be in desperate need of Godly apostolic/prophetic leadership during this time. As the geese who fly in formation in the shape of an arrowhead, and who continually make way for new leadership to take the lead, so must the Body now make way for Benjamin to take the lead.

Benjamin, who was the *last son* and the *smallest tribe,* is the last who will now become the first. He must now come forward to take the lead as servants who serve the Lord for His purposes in the last days, who lead His procession up to the Throne, *"There is little Benjamin their leader"* (Ps. 68:27).

During this time of trouble on Earth, many deceivers will come in the name of Jesus to deceive many (v. 4). In the last days it will become increasingly important to be able to discern and differentiate between those who have been sent by God from those who are sending themselves. A place of safety will be found with the Benjamites under the covering of their willingness to unite as one tribe on the side of righteousness.

Those who have been sent will also be recognized for their choice to remain silent. *As sheep before their shearers,* they will trust the Lord to be their defense (1 Pet. 2:23). The deceivers will easily be recognized by arrogance as they stand apart from the rest of the Body, self-righteously believing they are fighting on the side of God as they persecute and rail against those God has chosen as His vanguard.

> *"Therefore I am sending you prophets, wise men, and teachers. Some of them you will kill and crucify; others you will flog in your synagogues and pursue from town to town." Matthew 23:34*

It is never wise to get in the way of God's purposes, but this is an extremely dangerous time of history to be found resisting God or blocking the path to the fulfillment of His will. Judgment will fall on all who stand in the way of the Lord, who refuse to conform and give way for God's end-time purposes to now come forth.

Jesus spent Himself for three years on the twelve through whom He began His work of *building up His House.* He is now spending Himself on the 144,000 through whom He will finish this work. These men and women are not an elitist group of power-hungry egocentric leaders, but rather a tribe of slave servants who will pay an extremely high price to be called servants of the Lord.

Paul, who described himself many times as a bondservant of Christ, and served the Lord through many trials, came from the tribe of Benjamin. Jeremiah the prophet, who served as the Lord's voice to warn of the coming judgment, came from the tribe of Benjamin. This apostle and prophet portray a picture of the dimension of leadership called for in this hour. Mordecai, who refused to bow the knee to the enemy, stood for God against Haman, an antichrist-type figure, was from the tribe of Benjamin. Esther, who made the decision to lay down her life and said, "If I perish, I perish," was also from this tribe.

These great saints portray a picture of the last-day generation who will give everything and take everything thrown at them to complete the course and finish the race. The disciples of Christ all described themselves as *doulos*—slaves of Christ, *"Paul a servant,"*

"Peter a servant," "James a servant," and *"John a servant."* These men gave all for the Lord, including their lives.

Benjamin, the Servant, the Messenger, the Man Child, and the Branch, all represent Jesus in union with a tribe who *volunteer freely* on the Day of His Power. The second time Jesus comes will not be as the first when He came as *one* man representing the Father and Holy Spirit. The prophetic words that speak of Jesus as the Servant, the Messenger, etc. are all prophetic pictures of Jesus in the end times coming in union with *many brethren*.

The race through the time of Jacob's trouble and tribulation that comes to try the earth will be the hardest race ever run by the saints. Jesus said that He would cut it short for the elect's sake. Many, maybe unknowingly, have been training all their lives like Olympic athletes to run this one race—*the 200-cubit dash to the Return of Christ*. These runners have been trained in *fire* to run the *gauntlet of fire*.

These leaders are trained midwives who stand with the Body during this time of hard labor to bring forth 'The Christ'—the saints in Glory. *"A woman, when she is in labour has sorrow because her hour has come."* Her sorrow soon turns to joy after she has brought forth. The night of sorrow will end with joy in the morning when Christ shows up. The path ahead of us, to bring in the Great Harvest from the sea of humanity to the shore where Jesus is waiting is the distance now between us and Christ's Return in Glory. He is waiting with a Great Feast—the Feast of Tabernacles, to break our long fast apart from Him that began after He left. We have been eating at the Communion table as we have waited for Him to return (Lk. 22:18).

God is coming to firmly establish His leadership of the last days who will lead the Body through to the other side. He is now asking many to count the cost and to choose.

"If anyone comes to Me and does not hate his father and mother, wife and children, brothers and sisters, yes and his own

life also, he cannot be My disciple. And whoever does not bear his cross and come after Me cannot be My disciple. For which of you, intending to build a tower, does not sit down first and count the cost, whether he has enough to finish it—lest after he has laid the foundation, and is not able to finish, all who see it begin to mock him, saying, "this man began to build and was not able to finish." Or what king going to make war against another king, does not sit down first and consider whether he is able with ten thousand to meet him who comes against him with twenty thousand? Or else, while the other is still a great way off, he sends a delegation and asks for conditions of peace. So likewise, whoever of you does not forsake all that he has cannot be My disciple." Luke 14:25-33

As we ponder and deliberate over our answer to the Lord, certain things need to be taken into consideration. No man in his humanity has the ability or possesses any leadership qualities that will aid him in running this race. The task that lies ahead for God's leaders is a supernatural task that cannot be done outside of the Love of the Father and the Power and anointing of the Holy Spirit.

"Not by might nor by power, but by My Spirit," Saith the LORD of hosts. Who art thou, O great mountain? before Zerubbabel thou shalt become a plain: and he shall bring forth the headstone thereof with shoutings, crying, Grace, grace unto it." Zechariah 4:6

On the day that Jesus was baptized in the Jordan, He was baptized into both the love of His Father and the anointing and Power of the Spirit as preparation for the path that lay ahead of Him (Matt. 3:16-17). On the day of Pentecost, the apostles were also baptized into both, in preparation for the task that lay ahead of them.

There was a time when I thought that God had gone too far in what He was asking of me. He met me in my place of desperation and despair with His incredible love and told me that serving Him was *my choice*—that *I* was to decide whether I would willingly pay the price. I chose to say yes and to go on. I asked forgiveness for resentment, self-pity, and unbelief and wrote out a covenant with the Lord where I pledged with the Lord's help and with His strength to embrace the call fully, to be willing to pay the cost, the sacrifice and to pick up my cross and follow wholeheartedly after Him.

I realized that having done this, I no longer had any excuse for self-pity or to complain about anything as I had made my own choice. After a time of prayer, I opened my Bible and read:

"Lord who may dwell in your sanctuary? Who may live on your holy hill? He whose walk is blameless and who does what is righteous, who speaks the truth from his heart...who keeps his oath, even when it hurts." Psalm 15:1-4

I believe God was saying to me that He knew what it cost me to say yes, but also that He expects me to keep my oath even though it may continue to hurt.

Who is willing to say yes to the Lord, to trust Him to uphold and keep you through this time with His righteous Right Arm? Who is willing to drink His cup and be baptized with His baptism? Who will follow Him even though it may mean the cross? Who will be willing to face their pain to be healed and made whole to qualify to run this race? Who will say, Yes Lord, *"Here I am send me"?*

The baton is being passed to these 144,000 *last runners*, who will run the last mile of the race. They will be given renewed strength and power to finish the race and lead the Body through to the Promised Land. The Body desperately needs these leaders and must support them in every respect; the hour is calling for them to come forth.

"Gather to me my consecrated ones, who made a covenant with me by sacrifice." Psalm 50:5

The apostolic/prophetic builds and announces. They work together to build a house for the King as they announce and prepare the way for His Coming. It is time now for the Body to build the Most Holy Place for Christ's Return and it is now time to begin to prepare the Earth for the Coming of Christ. It is now time to prepare for the fulfillment of every vision.

> *"Son of man, what is the proverb that you people have about the land of Israel, which says, 'The days are prolonged, and every vision fails'? Tell them therefore, 'Thus says the LORD God: "I will lay this proverb to rest... But say to them, "The days are at hand, and the fulfilment of every vision. For no more there be any false vision or flattering divination...For I am the Lord I speak and the word which I speak will come to pass; it will no more be postponed, for in your days, O rebellious house, I will say the word and perform it," says the LORD GOD.'"* Ezekiel 12:22*

We do not know the Day when Jesus will return but, in the Spirit, the entire Body is feeling the urgency of the hour. It is now time to prepare for *the time*. The call on this dispensation and specifically this generation is to work with God to change history and finish *His story*. We do not know how long we have before Jesus returns, but the time we have *is exactly the time needed*, therefore no time can be wasted. God has given us a window of time and there is much work to be done. Elisha held Joash the king's hand on his bow and told him to open the east window and *shoot the arrow of the Lord's deliverance* through it (2 Kings 13:15). This is a picture of the Lord's hand now holding the hand of His leadership and saying to them:

> *You must open the east window of the Temple; through this window, you will receive revelation and knowledge, and an impartation of Power to equip you for the days of My coming. Shoot your arrows of deliverance and strike the enemy; continue to strike your arrows until you have destroyed them and see the Sun of righteousness arising from the east with healing in His wings.*

Chapter Twenty-One

THE FIRST SACRIFICE

"I beseech you therefore, brethren, by the mercies of God, that you present your bodies a living sacrifice, holy, acceptable to God, which is your reasonable service." Romans 12:1

In the fullness of time, with the culmination of history, the caliber of leadership within the Headstone generation will be represented by a company who have committed themselves to the Lord as living sacrifices. Through complete surrender, submission, and unwavering obedience, they transcend the constraints of the flesh, finding purpose solely in their commitment to Christ. Guided by the steps of their Commander, they willingly present their lives to fulfill His Divine purposes. Together they form the Vanguard of the Lord, a company of exceptionally skilled generals and soldiers dedicated to dismantling the strongholds of the enemy and guiding the saints into the Promised Land—the epoch of the Kingdom Age.

On the path to fullness, the *body* follows the *head* as it leads the way forward into Glory. The Headstone generation, positioned at the forefront, endures the greatest pressure, and confronts the most resistance on its relentless journey toward union in Christ. Positioned at the forefront, the Headstone becomes the initial target facing down the adversary's attempts to impede the birthing process. It confronts the many threats that seek to devour the emerging life at its inception before it can fully emerge into full stature (Rev. 12). The Headstone is a *firstfruit* unto God, a firstborn son—the *first male* to break open the womb (Lk.2:23). These are the *sons of God* the earth is in travail to see manifested.

The Headstone therefore represents the *first sacrifice* and endures the greatest attacks of the enemy. Like the head of an arrow, it suffers the greatest shocks at the point of contact with the enemy. Because of its willingness to suffer for the Lord's Passion, for His Bride, and for His purposes, this Headstone generation is holy to the Lord.

On the Day of the Lord—*the Day of His Power*, the 144,000 apostolic/prophetic leaders represented in the Headstone will be a firstfruit unto God as *the first sacrifice*. The Greek word for firstfruit is the word *aparche*, which means *the beginning of sacrifice*, or *the first sacrifice*. This company sings a new song having left behind the old ways and mindsets of religion and division:

> *"They sang as it were a new song before the throne...being firstfruits to God and to the lamb" Revelation 14:3*

To break through the mindsets and strongholds of the enemy standing in the way of Christ's return, the Headstone by its union with Christ, will move under the power of the *Breaker Anointing*. This anointing functions to make a way for God's people. It goes before, to break open the womb for God's purposes to be birthed; the break the bride's amniotic sac to release the rivers to flow, to break down barriers, and break open the way for the Body to break through into the Promised Land of the Kingdom reign of Christ.

> *"The one who breaks open will come up before them; they will break out, pass through the gate, and go out by it; their king will pass before them, with the Lord at their head." Micah 2:13*

The Head of the Body is not a place reserved for special people with special privileges; it is a place reserved for crucified people. Should anyone feel insignificant, left out, and desire a place in the forefront the answer is to *become a living sacrifice*. Die to everything you hold dear, your ambitions, plans, goals, and agendas. Be willing to walk through intense fires and deep waters, and very soon you will be out there at the forefront.

THE HEADSTONE

The Headstone necessitates conformity to the mind of Christ to be fortified against the assaults of the enemy, and to wield the wisdom required for leading and guiding the Body through the challenges that will come. Having undergone intense refinement in the crucible of fire and tribulation, the Headstone emerges with resilience, capable of withstanding immense pressure, a testament to its endurance and strength. They serve as exemplary leadership for others to follow.

> *"Behold, I have made your face strong against their faces, and your forehead strong against their foreheads. Like adamant stone, harder than flint, I have made your forehead..." Ezekiel 3:8*

Adamant stone, known for its unbreakable and utmost hardness, epitomizes resilience and steadfastness. The word adamant means *unyielding and resistant to persuasion*. Made from *adamant stone*, the Headstone is, therefore, able to resist the temptation to capitulate or compromise. It comes forth, through the Benjamin gate of *hard labor* (Gen.35:16).

God reveals His Son in these leaders, forged in the furnace of affliction. These tried and tested sons of God, having completed their obedience, undergo a transformation marked by foreheads of adamant stone (2 Cor 10:-6). The Name of the Lord is chiselled into their foreheads, as they stand resolute during great storms on the Earth.

"Then I looked, and behold, a Lamb standing on Mount Zion, and with Him one hundred and forty-four thousand, having His Father's name written on their foreheads." Revelation 14:1

As Israel prepared to leave the wilderness and the past behind, to cross over the Jordan and enter their inheritance, God ordained a Divine protocol for their travel (Josh.3:4). The priests, the leadership of that day, bore the Ark of the Lord on their shoulders. They went into the frigid waters of the Jordan, representing crucifixion and the embrace of the cross. The armed warriors then crossed over *ahead of the people.* Leadership goes first to break open the way. They break through resistance and smash through demonic barriers, and mindsets as they stand in the place of death bearing the Cross of Christ.

Through their obedience to God's instructions, a remarkable event unfolded as He parted the rushing waters, allowing them to pass through. Once everyone had crossed, Joshua directed the leaders to retrieve twelve stones from the river, creating a memorial for future generations. In doing so, God ensured that forthcoming generations would comprehend His ways and the significance of this miraculous event.

Following this, Joshua placed twelve stones in the middle of the Jordan, marking the spot where the "priests' feet stood firm" (Josh. 4:3). These priests demonstrated unwavering obedience to the Lord, standing steadfast against all resistance, resolute in their commitment to fulfill God's purpose and ensure the safe crossing of His people. Only after everyone had safely crossed did the priests exit the Jordan—*they were the last to do so.*

"So the priests who bore the ark stood amid the Jordan until everything was finished..." Joshua 4:10

This is a picture of apostolic resilience in those who are appointed to death. *"I will show him how many things he must suffer for My name's sake"* (Acts 9:16). They are appointed as living sacrifices that others may live (1 Cor.4:13).

"...God has put us apostles on display at the end of the procession. Like men condemned to die in the arena."
1Corinthians 4:9

The Lord gave me a revelation of a picture of the Titanic ship as the powerful denominational church heading on a collision course with the Rock. This gargantuan monolith the world calls the *church of God*, full of pride and arrogance, deceived into believing that it could not sink, was headed straight on a collision course with the Rock, that is Jesus Christ.

In this picture, I sensed the Lord revealing that as there was with the Titanic, there's currently a lack of adequately prepared lifeboats ready to rescue those in the waters. These lifeboats symbolize diverse gathering structures such as local churches, house churches, online churches, marketplace assemblies, or cell groups. All these should be poised to receive the wounded and rescue those drowning in disillusionment. Leaders play a vital role in preparing these lifeboats, ensuring people cross over into the welcoming and loving embrace of God the Father. God is shaking and rebuilding the foundation of His House and His Leaders need to anticipate not just a significant harvest of lost souls heading towards the Ark of Christ, but also a substantial migration of Christians seeking authentic Christianity.

These structures will function as lifeboats prepared for the hour, liberated from past mindsets and ready to serve the Master's *new work* in the new dynamic of the hour (Is. 43:19). Those who lead during this period will have traversed the journey, benefitted from lessons learned and be equipped to efficiently move and guide people through the process. Through trials and tests, they've honed their ability as guides to navigate the path of Christ in a walk of faith. God is in the process of preparing these warrior leaders to cross over and lead the harvest safely across the stormy waters representing the Cross, into the Kingdom age.

THE CROSSOVER

At the beginning of the building of the Temple of God, and each subsequent milestone in its construction, God orchestrated a massive invasion on earth. An awesome power surge of heavenly supernatural Power was released to initiate the *new work.* Great Power accompanied by signs and wonders was released through the time of Israel's Passover from captivity into God's purposes and throughout their journey in the wilderness.

At Pentecost, as the foundation of the Temple's superstructure was laid, tremendous power was once again unleashed, causing the entire building to shake. The Holy Spirit's Wind swept in with a rushing sound, and tongues of fire rested upon the disciples as the inauguration of the *new work* unfolded, accompanied by remarkable signs and wonders.

At the Feast of Tabernacles, when the foundation of the Headstone—the final phase of the Temple—is laid, an immense power will once more be unleashed to finalize the work in humanity and on Earth. This marks the *Day of God's Power,* where His people willingly offer themselves to construct this Holy Sanctuary for the Lord and serve as His ambassadors to the nations. The angelic host will be fully deployed to stand alongside the saints in the end-time battles, ensuring the emergence of the Headstone and the fulfillment of God's purposes. The armies of Heaven and Earth will move in a synergy called Mahanaim (See our book: *The Arising Army of God*).

Over the centuries, we have been steadily moving towards this significant event, but are we adequately prepared for the hour we are now called to? The question Paul asks arises: *"Who is sufficient for these things?"* The answer is clear—no one! No one is truly adequate to represent Christ to the world, to convey His wisdom with the love of Christ, devoid of all traces of arrogance and pride in a day of tremendous challenges.

THE HEADSTONE

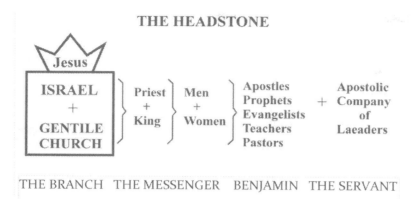

THE BRANCH   THE MESSENGER   BENJAMIN   THE SERVANT

This is a Day where humility must take precedence, where every knee will ultimately bow. Arrogance, characterized by presumption and self-importance, must be cast aside in the face of God's Holy work at hand.

Moses, due to the arrogance of presumption, found himself unable to enter the Promised Land when he struck the rock in anger, defying God's command. God's deep love for us no longer allows Him to tolerate such arrogance among His people. As we approach the end of time, for our protection, the God will treat us as beloved sons and daughters, disciplining us with increasing severity until we grasp the importance and significance of obedience.

"If you endure chastening, God deals with you as with sons; for what son is there whom a father does not chasten? But if you are without chastening, of which all have become partakers, then you are illegitimate and not sons. Furthermore, we have had human fathers who corrected us, and we paid them respect. Shall we not much more readily be in subjection to the Father of spirits and live? For they indeed for a few days chastened us as seemed best to them, but He for our profit, that we may be partakers of His holiness. Now no chastening seems to be joyful for the present, but painful; nevertheless, afterward, it yields the peaceable fruit of righteousness to those who have been trained by it." Hebrews 12:7

It is time to leave the captivity of Babylon brought on by pride, and return in the Spirit of humility to Jerusalem, the place of God's Heart and Mind on all matters concerning His Body. He will then begin to work through us to complete His Temple.

The Headstone, the Man Child, and the Messenger collectively embody Christ and an apostolic assembly of leaders in a profound Holy union.

> "And she brought forth a man child, who was to rule all nations with a rod of iron; and her child was caught up unto God and to His throne." Revelation 12:5 KJV

They are united in extraordinary power, filled with the Spirit without measure, and walking in harmony under the commanded blessing of God. The entire Earth anticipates the unveiling and emergence of these *sons of God*. Throughout history, we've witnessed glimpses of the Man Child, evolving, and maturing in the womb. Presently, we are in the midst of the birthing process, experiencing the unfolding events revealed in Revelation 12.

The name of Israel means *he will rule as God* and God's promise to the overcoming Assembly of His people, was power over the nations to *"rule with a rod of iron"* (Rev. 2:26-27). The Seat of God's Throne is the top of the mountain we have been climbing over *His-story*. The maturity of the Man Child in the *maturity of times*, places him securely on the seat of the Throne, far above all principalities and powers (Eph. 1:10).

Chapter Twenty-Two

BEHOLD HE COMES!

"Lift up your heads, O you gates! Lift up, you everlasting doors! And the King of glory shall come in. Who is this king of glory? The Lord of hosts, He is the King of glory." Psalm 24:9-10

J esus discouraged His disciples from looking to dates but He was also angry with the Pharisees for not discerning the signs of the times (Matt. 16:3). Because of their unbelief and lack of faith, the Pharisees could not discern the times they were living in. In his epistle to the Thessalonians, Paul said that he didn't need to write about *times* and *seasons* as it was known that the Day of the Lord would come as a thief in the night. Both words 'times' and 'seasons' are translated from the Greek word *kairos*, which means *the appointed time*. But Paul goes on to tell them:

> *"For when they say, "Peace and safety!" then sudden destruction comes upon them, as labour pains upon a pregnant woman. And they shall not escape. But you, brethren, are not in darkness, so that this Day should overtake you as a thief...Therefore let us not sleep, as others do, but let us watch and be sober." 1 Thessalonians 5:3-4*

The direction and purposes of God are about to take a sharp turn. God has been intently focusing His attention on His leaders and His army. He has been fine-tuning, oiling, cleaning, and testing His instruments of war. He is about to fire these weapons, His flames of fire, scattering them like napalm across the Earth.

When the Glory comes, so does the judgment of God on sin. God has been preparing many Josephs and Joseph churches, who have paid the price to *go ahead to preserve life*. They have been in pits and prisons, misunderstood and persecuted as part of their preparation and training for becoming the administrators of food in times of famine. In Joseph's Day, the world had to come to Joseph to get food. This was the only place where food was available. God has been storing food in 'cities' all over the world. These are people and churches that have become beachheads or bases of operations for the Lord and carriers of His Flame.

The individuals and the churches who have been like the five wise virgins, faithfully filling up their lamps with oil, will be the ones with sufficient oil to keep them through this time. The five wise virgins not only filled their lamps they also filled up extra jars, *"The wise however took oil in jars along with their lamps"* (Matt. 25:4 NIV). Not only were they wise, but we can understand from this passage that they had a great hunger and passion for God and were greedy for His Presence and His anointing.

We are now being prepared for times of great Glory and times of great darkness. Both are coming at the same time (Is. 60:1). The Glory of God is coming surrounded by great storms and turbulence. But these storms will serve God's purposes to clear a path for Him. Sweeping judgments will come that will shake the Earth free of demonic infiltration as the heavenly hosts prepare to reap the Earth of this vile and abominable harvest (Rev. 14:18).

> *"Plague went before Him, pestilence followed his steps. He stood and shook the earth; He looked, and made the nations tremble." Habbakuk 3:5-6 NIV*

Eyes will be opened to understand the deception that the world has lived under and to see the *truth*. We are waiting for the fire to fall. The union of prayer that will be issued from the birthing of the Headstone of the Body will ascend as a Holy fragrance before the Throne and have great power with God. In Revelation chapter 8, there was silence in Heaven for half an hour.

The angel with the golden censor then came before the altar to offer up with the incense, the prayers of all the saints. He then took the censer, filled it with fire, and threw it to the Earth. Prayer has been ascending into Heaven from across the Earth like never before in history and the bowls are getting full.

As they did in the book of Acts, the apostles and prophets are the flame-throwers who will light up the Earth in revival fire when God sees that the Bride has been made ready and is positioned securely. The apostles and prophets are being established and set in place to prepare a wineskin that will withstand the burden of the hour without tearing. The last stages of the work to complete the Temple are beginning to prepare for His Return. We are steadily and resolutely moving towards the consummation of all things. We are approaching the end of an exceptionally long road and an extremely hard race. My prayer is that we will all have the strength and the courage to run the race set before us to finish the work, for Jesus said that a day would come when no one would be able to work.

"I must work the works of Him who sent Me while it is day; the night is coming when no one can work." John 9:4

In the same way that David made all the preparations and provisions for the building of the Temple of God, Jesus made all the preparations and provisions for the Temple to be *completed.*

"Indeed I have taken much trouble to prepare for the house of the LORD one hundred thousand talents of gold and one million talents of silver, and bronze and iron beyond measure, for it is so abundant. I have prepared timber and stone also, and you may add to them. Moreover there are workmen with you in abundance: woodsmen and stonecutters, and all types of skillful men for every kind of work. Of gold and silver and bronze and iron there is no limit. Arise and begin working, and the LORD be with you." 1 Chronicle 22:14-16

God has been preparing His skilled workers—Intercessors, leaders, churches, and ministries: specialists in every field of building work, *"all types of skillful men"* and women, each one having their part to contribute, important the completion of the House. The wine and the oil are being prepared to be poured out, to sustain and equip all the workers to complete the building, and for the procession to bring the Ark of His Presence into the Sanctuary.

"Now set your heart and your soul to seek the LORD your God. Therefore arise and build the sanctuary of the LORD God, to bring the ark of the covenant of the LORD and the holy articles of God into the house that is to be built for the name of the LORD." 1 Chronicles: 22:19

The *Day of His Power* is a period when the Power of God will be released on the Earth and through man on a level that has never been seen before. This Power will be released to prepare the way for His coming and will steadily increase in strength until it reaches its fullness at the Return of Christ.

God now has beachheads or 'cities' strategically placed all over the Earth, prepared and positioned for revival. At the appointed time, these 'cities' will be flooded with the Light of His Glory in preparation for His Return. The lever to switch on these floodlights of revival fire and to release the River to flow again in *fullness* has been placed in the City of Jerusalem, Israel. Why Jerusalem? Jerusalem is the location of the Cross of Jesus, fulfilling the Passover Feast. After His resurrection, Jesus told the disciples to tarry and *wait in Jerusalem* until they were endued with power from on High! Every milestone in God's building work has been birthed within Jerusalem. God will honor what He started in Jerusalem—the City of God. Revival Fire will mark the cities that have become one in heart with Israel.

In the end, the Body of Christ will arise to the Stature and measure, of the fullness of deity. The headwaters of this River will flow from Israel, the Head—the Seat of His Throne—down through the belly of His Church and out to the nations, covering the Earth with the *"...knowledge of the Glory of the LORD as the waters cover the sea."*

The Commanded Blessing was poured out as oil upon the head of Aaron the high priest, a picture of Israel. At the appointed time God will pull the lever and flood the Earth with revival waters. There will be an explosion out of Jerusalem that will rock and shake the entire face of the Earth.

As the signs of the age to come begin to manifest in our midst, Hebrews 6:5 resounds with a call to taste the goodness of the Word of God and experience the powers *of the coming age.* This anticipation ushers in an expectation of the signs and wonders that will increase, mirroring Jesus' declaration that *"the kingdom of God has come upon you."*

The celestial and terrestrial realms are converging, as God's grand design unfolds, uniting everything in Heaven and on Earth in Christ. Ephesians 1:9 unveils the mystery of His will, purposed in Christ for the great climax of the ages, when all things, both in Heaven and on Earth, will be brought together under Christ's Lordship. There are unmistakable signs now heralding the arrival of His Kingdom.

The current times call for a profound shift that ushers in the Great Awakening. Existing structures must either adapt to the winds of change that are blowing or risk being dismantled. Carnal works will inevitably be consumed in the refining fire of change, and it is only a matter of time until *the day* reveals the true nature of all our works.

It is time to prepare the Headstone Sanctuary to bring the Ark to its place of Rest! *To everything, there is a season and a time for every purpose.* The time has come for Jews and Gentiles to work together to build the Temple of the Lord according to God's Blueprint and bring in the Ark of His Presence.

1 Corinthians 3:10 underscores the importance of building on the unshakable foundation of Jesus Christ. How we build upon this foundation matters: whether with gold, silver, precious stones, or with wood, hay, or straw. The day will expose the authenticity of our efforts, for each work will be tested by fire. Though some may suffer loss, they will be saved, as if escaping through flames.

In parallel with John the Baptist's call to repentance, as a precursor to Christ's first coming, a renewed message of repentance now resounds in preparation for His second coming. Matthew 3:2 announces the nearness of God's Kingdom and echoes the sound that it is *fast approaching.*

Nations and cities positioned across the globe, are being prepared for His return, and are being called to account as saints strategize in preparation for the arrival of the King. In a fashion reminiscent of biblical times, messengers are being sent forth, and pioneers are being dispatched ahead of His arrival.

When Jesus descended to the lowest regions and then ascended to the Throne He filled His Body with His *Zoe* Life—*the knowledge of Himself and the Glory of His Presence*—beginning from the soles of His feet from where He ascended, to the place of His Throne—*He declared it was finished!* Isaiah declared that in the last days, the earth would be full of the knowledge of the LORD *(11:9).* Habakkuk declared that the Earth would be full of the knowledge of *the glory* of the LORD. The light of the knowledge of God's Glory is displayed in the face of Jesus (2 Cor. 4:6).

In a moment of intense intercession, a friend received a vivid image from the Lord—a row of clocks, each one falling one by one. As the last clock fell, three remarkably large and intensely bright floodlights illuminated from behind. The revelation is profound: in the *conclusion of time,* after the Headstone is in place and the Temple completed, Jesus returns and is crowned King. At that time, floodlights of the Glory of Father, Son, and Holy Spirit will radiate from the Temple, illuminating it with Divine light, to flood the Earth with heavenly Glory.

"The city had no need of the sun or of the moon to shine in it, for the glory of God illuminated it. The Lamb is its light."
Revelation 21:23

Jesus is the Light of the world. God is about to turn on the Lights in His House and is saying to His people to arise and shine for the hour of Light has come! The people who walk in darkness will see a Great Light (Matt. 4:16). The Earth will be flooded with the Glory of God emanating from the King and through His Glorified Saints.

According to Revelation 21:23, the Lamb is the Light of the City of God ... *And the name of the city from that day shall be Yahweh Shamah:* THE LORD IS THERE!

In the year that arrogance perished, and sin was abandoned:

"I saw the Lord sitting on a throne, high and lifted up,
and the train of His robe filled the temple.
Above it stood seraphim, each one had six wings:
With two he covered his face, with two he covered his
feet, and with two he flew. And one cried to another and said:
"Holy, holy, holy is the LORD of hosts;
the whole earth is full of His glory!"
And the posts of the door were shaken...
and the house was filled with smoke."
Isaiah 6:1-4

Behold He Comes!

Chapter Twenty-Three

EVEN SO, COME!

"This same Jesus, who was taken up from you into heaven, will so come in like manner as you saw Him go into heaven." Acts 1:11

Jesus is the magnificent obsession of devoted souls throughout the ages! He is the expressed image of the invisible God, the bright Morning Star who will return in glory—what an incredible day to be alive! What a privilege to be chosen for this hour, to belong to the generation who will see the closing of an era and prepare the way for the coming of the King of kings.

> *"Blessed are the eyes which see the things you see; for I tell you that many prophets and kings have desired to see what you see, and have not seen it, and to hear what you hear, and have not heard it." Luke 10:24*

This generation is walking through and living out the fulfillment of prophecies written in the Word of God thousands of years ago. We are seeing events take place that the prophets saw from a great distance. As the disciples and their generation were chosen and blessed to see the Messiah and to be the witnesses of the unfolding of great prophetic events, so is this generation chosen and honored to be participants in the work to open the Gates to the King of kings and be witnesses of His return in Glory.

History, in essence, is *His Story*, told through the lives of sons and daughters, and the choices humanity has made whether in obedience or disobedience to His Word. It unfolds through the valleys and over the mountains traversed by humanity, through the joys and sorrows that constitute and shape life, and through the remarkable triumphs and tragic defeats the Earth has endured. His Story continues to unfold in this present hour on Earth. It is closely observed by Heaven, as it marks the culmination of all things in Christ. The summing up of all things in Him is beginning, and preparations for His Return are being set in place.

Many will scoff at any of these things coming to pass, but God says that His Word will be fulfilled, and nothing can change that, as His Word stands forever (1 Pet. 1:25). The Lord showed me a picture of an armored tank, representing *The Word of God*. This tank was moving very slowly but steadily across the desert sands of time. Throughout its journey, voices were raised in protest saying this or that could never be. However, the tank kept going! Some tried to put up a fight and get in its way, but the tank ran right over them and... *kept on going.*

In the nineteenth century and before that time, many voices declared that God was finished with Israel saying that the Church was the new Israel... *but the tank just kept going.* Voices declared that Israel would never again be a nation, that the land was just a dried-up piece of desert land, *but the tank simply kept on going.* When Israel became a nation once again and the desert began to blossom and bloom after two thousand years, voices around the world were raised in angry protest, but *the tank ignored their protestations and just kept going.*

Every Word that God has spoken will be fulfilled! The King of kings will return! He will reign in righteousness. The government shall rest upon His shoulders. Of the increase of His government, there shall be no end. His Glory will cover the Earth as the waters cover the sea. All nations will call Him Blessed and will come to worship Him. He was born from the womb of a virgin, and He will return in Glory as the conquering King.

"And behold you will conceive in your womb and bring forth a Son, and shall call His Name JESUS. He will be great, and will be

called the Son of the Highest; and the Lord God will give Him the throne of His father David. And He will reign over the house of Jacob forever, and of His kingdom there will be no end." Luke 1:31-33

The Jewish people believe the Messiah will enter Jerusalem by the Eastern Gate, also corroborated by Scripture.

"Afterward he brought me to the gate that faces toward the east. And behold the glory of the God of Israel came from the way of the east. His voice was like the sound of many waters; and the earth shone with His glory... And the glory of the Lord came into the temple by the way of the gate, which faces toward the east. The Spirit lifted me up and brought into the inner court; and behold, the glory of the Lord filled the temple." Ezekiel 43:1-5

There are seven steps leading to each Gate of the last day Temple, as described in Ezekiel 40:22. The saints of God have embarked on the Great Journey through time, ascending the seven steps of the Mountain of God. We have now arrived at the step of the seventh thousand year of His handiwork, having progressed through seven dispensations, to His seventh Dwelling Place, for a great celebration at the *seventh Feast*—a transcendent celebration given for the completion of the Journey and of God's surpassing work.

Throughout this journey, the cloud of His Presence has guided our movements, signaling the times when we have paused, as He patiently waited for us to reach His ultimate destination and final resting place—a Sanctuary where we dwell with Him for all eternity.

Jesus has been building the House of the Lord, He has been climbing these seven steps with us, along with His Father and the Holy Spirit, and will enter in Glory from the East. Yahweh—the Trinity of the Godhead, will enter through the Eastern Gate to take His Seat on the Throne of David, His final place of rest, as the

Great Journey through the *Story of the Ages* comes to its conclusion.

In the book of Ezekiel, the angel measured off four levels of water, four representing the completion of the New Creation in the Fullness of God. The water levels have been rising slowly over time as we have entered greater knowledge and understanding of our Lord. Like Ezekiel's River, the water levels began at the ankles, then rose to the knees, rose again to the waist, and then covered *the head*. These four stages correspond with each significant stage of the building of *The Christ*. As the Body was being drawn into the depths of God, into higher levels of the knowledge of God, from the natural into the Spiritual depths of the fullness of Christ, the ability to stand on natural ground was slowly being removed.

This River of the fullness of all that is God—the knowledge of His being, knowledge of His ways, and knowledge of the Glory of His Presence, flows out from this final Temple in its fullness, from the place of His Throne. This Temple representing His people in union with the Son, must be built and constructed according to the Heavenly pattern before the River of God can be released to flow in its fullness of Power.

The River signifies the fullness of the Son—it embodies the full dynamic of His Life. Originating *in Him*, it streams forth from the Throne of His heart to ours, extending its reach to all of humanity. As *the Israel of God*, resting as dew on the nations of the Earth grows up into the fullness of Christ, His Life—the River, will be increasing in volume, Power, and strength to cover the Earth as the waters cover the sea. It will surge with increasing volume, power, and strength, eventually covering and enveloping the entire Earth.

Throughout history, Israel has served as the conduit for God's blessings to the Earth. Every significant event had its roots in Israel. The River of Living Water commenced its flow at Pentecost *out of Jerusalem*. As all obstacles of sin in its way are destroyed, this River is destined to be unleashed like a tidal wave, emanating once again from Jerusalem—the heart and seat of God's Throne.

Positioned in a Spiritual prophetic moment, Jesus declared the eruption of this River out of the womb of His people on the *last and great day of the Feast of Tabernacles (Jn. 7:37).* Jewish people, whether consciously or unconsciously, have been steadily returning home from all the nations of the world in anticipation of this momentous occurrence and the world transforming event of Messiah's Return home *to Jerusalem.*

In one of the most holy and beautiful worship moments I've ever encountered, the worship leader was given a vision of a red carpet being rolled up. This initially puzzled us, as red carpets are typically rolled *out.* During a time of prayer, the Lord clarified the vision by showing me an image of someone preparing to move from their home, packing up their belongings, and rolling up the carpet. I believe the Lord was illustrating the nearness of His coming and the permanence of His stay. The sincere and refined worship of God's children, expressing our love and adoration for Him, will be the red carpet *rolled out* for the Return of our King.

Since the foundation of the Earth, God has been constructing a dwelling place for Himself—a House to bear His name. The construction of *Yahweh's House* or *The Christ,* has been an ongoing process, advancing progressively over the centuries. The foundation was established in Israel, as *"the place of My feet"* and will reach completion in Israel, *"the place of My throne,"* where God will manifest His Glory in fullness.

Ephesians 4:8-10 takes into view the birth and full formation of the Body of Christ from Jerusalem—from His feet up to His Head He filled the *whole vessel.* This passage is quoted from Psalm 68:18 and looks to the completion of the Temple and the celebration of the procession up to Jerusalem to seat the King of Glory in His final place of rest. In Him, there are many prepared mansions for all who belong to Him.

"Let God arise, let His enemies be scattered...They have seen Your procession, O God, the procession of my God, my King, into the sanctuary. The singers went before, the players on instruments followed after..." Psalm 68:1, 24-25

The Temple, the Man Child, the Bride, the Messenger, the Branch, the Servant, the House, the Israel of God, the Ekklesia, and Jerusalem—the City of the Living God—are all images portraying the union of Jesus with His saints. Each depiction serves to represent, reveal, and impart distinct aspects and characteristics of the Lord within the expansive universe that is our God—Creator of stars and the Universe.

The Body of Christ that is the Temple of God must now be found positioned facing eastward in anticipation of the return of the King. For the Gentile Church, the focal point is the Eastern Gate, that is Israel. We must collaborate in obedience to God, to prepare this *Beautiful Gate* through which the Lord will make His triumphant return in Glory.

Let all eyes be fixed on Jesus, the Head, with watchful obedience, to observe the extraordinary unveiling of the Majesty Glory of *The Christ*. Like the sun, His rising will occur in the east, emerging from the womb of the dawn during the Day of His Power when He comes to reign in Glory over all the Kingdoms of the Earth.

"Proclaim the power of God whose majesty is over Israel. Whose power is in the skies. You are awesome, O God, in Your sanctuary; the God of Israel gives power and strength to His people. Praise be to God." Psalm 68 NIV

This book has been about *the beginning* and *the end* of the Great Journey of the Story of Christ played out through the centuries—the *Alpha and the Omega*. The Journey began in the womb of the wilderness, where foundations were laid in a chosen people, and where the Lord began the marvellous work of the creation of His Bride:

"And when I passed by you and saw you struggling in your own blood, I said to you in your blood, 'Live!' Yes, I said to you in your blood, 'Live!' I made you thrive like a plant in the field; and you grew, matured, and became very beautiful. Your breasts were formed, your hair grew, but you were naked and bare. "When I passed by you again and looked upon you, indeed your time was the time of love; so I spread My wing over you and covered your nakedness. Yes, I swore an oath to you and entered into a covenant with you, and you became Mine, says the Lord GOD." Ezekiel 16:6-8

Throughout history, we have witnessed the development and continual growth of His Bride, steadily maturing toward completeness. The long great journey is now approaching its conclusion, arriving at the season of fulfillment and fullness. All of creation is on edge, in eager anticipation of the moment when the Bridegroom will come for His Bride and find rest with her in His Holy Temple. The procession up to Jerusalem, leading to the Temple of God, and the grand celebration of the marriage between the Bridegroom and the Bride—*is soon to begin!*

"Promise me, O women of Jerusalem, not to awaken love until the time is right." Song of Songs 8:4 NLT

"Promise me, brides-to-be, by the gentle gazelles and delicate deer, that you'll not disturb my love until he is ready to arise." TPT

The Wedding Feast approaches, and the time to *awaken Love* is upon us. The angels tremble with anticipation. The Father looks on with pride and joy in His Heart. The Spirit makes the final preparations. The Son waits. The Bridegroom is waiting patiently for the Word from His Father that says *"It is time."* This is a unique time in history when both Jew and Gentile together, longingly await the coming of their Messiah King.

When Solomon completed the building of the Temple, he brought all the dedicated things, the silver, the gold, and all the furnishings, and placed them in the treasuries of God's Temple. This speaks of the Harvest, God's children who are the treasures of His heart. Solomon then summoned all the elders of Israel and the heads of all the tribes to the Feast of Tabernacles to bring in the *Ark of God*. All the worshipers and the musicians were present as one hundred and twenty priests sounded the trumpets of offerings of praise and thanksgiving to Almighty God (2 Chron. 5:1).

Solomon, the royal son, then dedicated the Temple to the Lord in prayer. When He was finished praying, fire came down from Heaven, and the Glory of the Lord filled the Temple. The priests could not enter the House because of the Glory that had filled the Lord's House.

"When all the children of Israel saw how the fire came down, and the Glory of the Lord on the temple, they bowed their faces to the ground on the pavement, and worshiped and praised the Lord saying: "For He is good, For His mercy endures forever."

Now therefore,

Arise, O Lord God, to your resting place,

You and the ark of Your strength.

2 Chronicles 7:3, 6:41

"He who testifies to these things says,

"Surely I am coming quickly." Amen.

Revelation 22:20

Even so, come, Lord Jesus!

ABOUT THE AUTHOR

In 1993, Faith Marie Baczko experienced a life-altering encounter with the Lord in her downtown Toronto apartment. Responding to divine guidance, she made a courageous decision to leave behind her career as a fashion designer, along with the store she had recently opened in the heart of Toronto. When she sought direction from the Lord, His response was clear: "Write." Despite lacking any prior writing experience or natural ability, Faith chose to trust God's calling and obediently followed His lead.

Tragedy struck in 2006 when Faith lost her son in a devastating car accident. In the aftermath, the Lord blessed her with a partner and husband. Shortly after their marriage, Faith established Headstone Ministries to facilitate her ministry to the Lord. Her deep passion revolves around aligning the House of God with the Plumb line of Christ and helping believers rise to their full potential in Christ to prepare the way for the Lord.

Faith Marie Baczko currently serves as the President of Faith Marie Baczko Ministries, a Ministry firmly rooted in God's purposes and plans. Her entrepreneurial and pioneering spirit continually drives her to break new ground. Faith is not only a prophetic teacher but also a bearer of profound revelations that mobilize, equip, and fortify the Body of Christ for this pivotal moment in history. She maintains a close association with Apostle Dr. Felipe Gonzalez, the Founder and leader of Beraca Church in Toronto, Ontario, and Apostle Carol McLean Founder of Jehovah Jireh Christian Ministries.

Faith is an accomplished author and has been a regular contributor to the Elijah List and Charisma Magazine. As an international speaker, she harbors a profound desire for the Army of God to rise with fervor and power. Her life sets an inspiring example, urging others to pursue Christ with unwavering dedication. Faith has organized numerous conferences and schools in South America, fostering enduring relationships with pastors and leaders. Several of her books are available in Spanish, making her insight accessible to a broader audience.

Having sat at the Lord's feet for many years receiving the revelation on the Headstone of the Temple of God, He has now released her to bring this timely word, to the Body of Christ. Like the women at the tomb, she has also received the command to, *"Go and tell..."* (Matt. 28).

Faith Marie Baczko is available for speaking engagements, and to hold schools & seminars focused on:

> ➢ The significance of Israel in God's purposes as the beginning and completion of His transcendent plan on Earth.
> ➢ The significance of God's plan for women in the last days for birthing the strategic purposes of God.
> ➢ Becoming ready as the Bride through healing and deliverance.
> ➢ The Power and anointing of the Headstone generation in the work to sum up all things in Christ.

For more information, please contact us at:

Website: www.faithmariebaczko.ca
Email: contact@faithmariebaczko.ca

THE HEADSTONE SERIES

Israel My Son: Jerusalem My Beloved

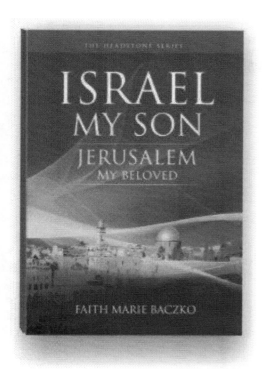

Israel My Son reveals the transcendent plan of God for Mankind, birthed through the nation of Israel. From before the foundation of the world, God intended that His plan for the Salvation of mankind be centred and administered in and through Israel, as the Word of God says, "...salvation is of the Jews" (John 4:22). The Spiritual Promised Land of Christ and the natural land of Israel became forever intertwined in the purposes of God beginning with Abraham's Obedience and completed in Christ.

A proper understanding of the significance of Israel to the counsels of God provides access to keys allowing us to apprehend the fullness of God's comprehensive plan, and the facility to be aligned with His purposes in this hour, for our nations. Israel My Son is a key to understanding our Hebraic roots, and how our identity is shaped as it relates to God's comprehensive plan.

If you are Christ's then this book is important for you as Jesus is the King of *the Israel of God,* who will reign eternally in Jerusalem. From the beginning to the end, it reveals key features of the greatest story ever told, without which major parts of the panoramic landscape of God's vision are obscured, producing many errors of interpretation.

FOUNDATIONS OF KINGDOM LEADERSHIP

Foundations of Leadership!

Establishing a secured foundation rooted in God's precepts, that mirror the transcendent life of Christ, is the prerequisite for effective Kingdom Leadership. This is particularly important at this pivotal juncture of history. The trumpet call for an army of authentic leaders to rise and embrace their rightful positions is resonating powerfully across the Global body of Christ.

In the current epoch, the demand for exceptional leadership has never been more pressing. Leaders navigating these turbulent times are needed at the forefront of addressing uncertainty and distinct challenges. Extraordinary leaders are indispensable as guides through tumultuous seasons of change.

Effective Kingdom Leadership becomes a beacon during times of uncertainty, offering steadfast and unwavering light. It requires not only the ability to navigate complexities but also the resilience to foster growth and transformation in God's people. As leaders navigate these challenging waters, they draw vision from the Life of Christ, embodying His virtues of compassion, wisdom, and servant-hearted leadership.

Hear the Trumpet Call to Leadership! Rise and be Counted in the Hour You Have Been Created For!

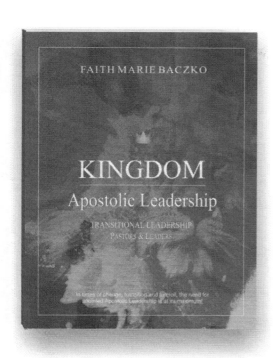

KINGDOM APOSTOLIC LEADERSHIP

TRANSITIONAL LEADERSHIP

Understanding the Dynamic of Transitional Leadership in the Overlap Season of Transcendent Change!

COMING SOON!

Manufactured by Amazon.ca
Bolton, ON